Find Your Voice

'David Oliver has written a clear and compelling case for the wise use of the gift of prophecy both inside and outside the church. I commend this book to anyone who eagerly desires the spiritual gifts, especially the gift of prophecy (1 Corinthians 14.1).'

Dr Mark Stibbe, Vicar of St Andrew's Chorleywood, England

'This book is personal, practical and prophetic. An excellent book: full of simple, helpful and practical ways of making prophecy available to all. I wholeheartedly recommend buying, reading and using this book either on your own or in a small group. I loved the personal stories, which demystify the prophetic and make it available to all.'

Mark Melluish, Vicar of St Paul's Ealing
and on the leadership team of New Wine

'The church has had laryngitis for far too long! David Oliver helps it to get its voice back with this excellent book. Dave has an equipping prophetic ministry and is someone with whom I have worked in many nations. What he is writing about works if you mix faith with action! Try it and enjoy the adventure with God.'

Dave Richards, Salt and Light

'This is an excellent practical book for those developing a prophetic gift and for those with the leadership responsibility to oversee that gift. The section on the use of the gift in our everyday working lives was full of helpful insight as well as a contagious enthusiasm.'

David Devenish, New Frontiers, England

Find Your Voice

Developing the Prophetic
in You and Your Church

David Oliver

Authentic

Copyright © 2007 David Oliver

18 17 16 15 14 13 12   8 7 6 5 4 3 2

First published 2007 by Authentic Media
Reprinted 2012 by Authentic Media Limited
52 Presley Way, Crownhill, Milton Keynes, MK8 0ES
www.authenticmedia.co.uk

British Library Cataloguing in Publication Data
A catalogue record for this book is available from the British Library

ISBN 978-1-86024-601-2

Cover design by David Lund Design
Typeset by Waverley Typesetters, Fakenham, Norfolk
Printed in Great Britain by
CPI Group (UK) Ltd, Croydon, CR0 4YY

Contents

Acknowledgement

My thanks to Alan Mann who has helped to craft the words. He has shaped each chapter into a facet so that the whole thing takes on a better shape and shines with a clearer light.

Preface

The evangelical and charismatic world is increasingly encouraging its members to prophesy, and many prophets are emerging. Churches have a range of experiences. Some churches are frightened of the gift, and uncomfortable in dealing with the individuals involved. Others have experienced great benefit and are looking for ways to develop and release their gifted members further. Many individuals are desperate to grow in their gift but are unsure how.

One thing is certain: the heart of God and the promise of God in Scripture are that in these days prophetic activity should be common, and it should be doing all of us good – individuals and churches alike.

This book attempts to unpack this gift practically for everyone, regardless of experience, to deal with some of the common problems that crop up, and to help with practical tools in the area of supernatural hearing, seeing and speaking. It approaches this at three levels:

- The church in general: 'Everyone can prophesy' – we can all have a go regularly
- Gifted prophetic people and those who may become 'Ephesians 4 prophets'
- Church leaders who have to live with the blessings and challenges that all this brings

It aims to answer many of the commonly asked questions. It seeks to inspire and equip all of us to have a go. It looks to supercharge already gifted prophetic people in developing their gifting, and provides many practical keys to do just that.

It offers tools for weighing prophetic words, so that church leaders and prophesying people alike can learn without fear or embarrassment to discern regularly what was of God, what was their own opinion and what was a mixture of the two.

Above all, the book is designed to encourage us to see more, hear more and bring more of the prophetic word. It will encourage us to develop our gifting, to reach out in faith for more, and to seek help from – and give help to – others in the process.

1

Everyone Can Prophesy

I shall never forget the night. All the men in our church had gathered together. Opening his Bible, the leader read these words:

> For you can all prophesy in turn so that everyone may be instructed and encouraged. (1 Cor. 14:31)

Then he looked up from his Bible, scanned the room and asked, 'How many of you believe this really is the Word of God?'

After a thoughtful silence, one by one, hands went up and agreeing heads nodded. Then, with a grin on his face, and to the group's mild surprise, he slowly and deliberately produced a key, locking the door of the room in which we were gathered.

'If you and I really do believe this is the Word of God,' he continued, 'we are not going home until everyone has prophesied tonight. We are going to encourage one another until we have fulfilled our part in this Scripture.'

A buzz of apprehension and excitement went through the group. The leader explained carefully what prophecy could include, and what to expect, and then we began.

To my amazement, every single man in turn did indeed prophesy that night. From the least educated to the most sophisticated, no one missed out. Our spirits were strengthened, our faith uplifted and our hearts encouraged. And as we prophesied, some of us had broad smiles, while others had tears in their eyes. Something powerful was released into the lives of those men that night. We were all in awe of God, for we all knew that we were changed for ever by that simple act.

Recently I was chatting to a friend of mine, Chris, who I believe has a well-developed prophetic gift. Intrigued, I asked him how he first discovered that he had such a gift. What interested me most was that he related a similar story to my own, even pointing to a verse from the same chapter in Scripture.

Chris had travelled with a group of around one hundred young people from Basingstoke Community Church to a weekend retreat on the Medina River in the Isle of Wight. On the Saturday night, the leadership addressed those present with this challenge:

'1 Corinthians 14:26 says. "When you come together, everyone has a hymn, or a word of instruction, a revelation, a tongue or an interpretation. All of these must be done for the strengthening of the church." Therefore, during our time together in the morning, we would like everybody to bring a verbal contribution. We don't mean prayers or Bible readings but gifts of the Spirit, like those Paul mentions here.'

The young people spent that Saturday night praying for each other and seeking God.

At breakfast the next morning, there was a mixture of apprehension and excitement. Some were unsure what would happen, and if truth be told, were a little fearful. Others thought they were facing no real challenge and had the bravado to match. But that Sunday morning, both the bold and the timid contributed, many prophetically.

The impact on the group was life-changing. There was an outpouring of commitment to God and the majority of that group, some twenty years on, are still regularly using gifts that were discovered and released that day in church gatherings and even their places of work. Many of them have since travelled on mission trips, while some have served on a long-term basis in China, Uganda, Burundi and other countries.

The promised generation

The reason why these two stories can happen, and should indeed happen all over the world (in your church and my church, in your daily life and my daily life), is because God promised it would happen.

I guess most of us reading this are aware that we are a unique and privileged generation. Some missiologists have suggested that in the last twenty-five years Christians have read more, experienced more and heard more about the Holy Spirit than in the rest of church history.

Though we are a privileged generation, we have to return to the ninth century BC to find the roots of that blessing in God's Word given through the prophet Joel:

> 'I will pour out my Spirit on all people. Your sons and daughters will prophesy, your old men will dream dreams, your young men will see visions. Even on my servants, both men and women, I will pour out my Spirit in those days.' (Joel 2:28–29)

Nine centuries later the fulfilment of this prophecy begins. On the day of Pentecost, Peter, emboldened by the Spirit of God, quotes these words and gives us a clear statement about their present application and the reason for his own and his companions' behaviour:

> 'Let me explain this to you; listen carefully to what I say. These men are not drunk, as you suppose. It's only nine in

the morning! No, this is what was spoken by the prophet Joel: "In the last days, God says, I will pour out my spirit on all people. Your sons and daughters will prophesy, your young men will see visions, your old men will dream dreams. Even on my servants, both men and women, I will pour out my Spirit in those days, and they will prophesy." ... God has raised this Jesus to life, and we are all witnesses of the fact. Exalted to the right hand of God, he has received from the Father the promised Holy Spirit and has poured out what you now see and hear.' (Acts 2:14–18, 32–33)

Pentecost, however, was not a one-off event. The promise was not just for nine o'clock that first-century morning. At the heart of Joel's prophecy, and of its unpacking by Peter, is a promise that reaches into the twenty-first century, to you and me, to our friends and to our children. This age – our age – is the age of the Holy Spirit: a God-guaranteed prophetic age.

What can easily be missed when reading this passage in our English translations, however, is that not only is the promise for now as well as for then, but, as the Greek language in which Acts was originally written clearly implies, prophecy is to be used frequently. As God's prophetically-privileged people we are to be characterised by regular prophetic activity.

I also find these scriptures enlightening and encouraging for our politically correct world, because they are totally inclusive. They are neither sexist nor ageist. There are no privileges for the economically well off or the socially successful. The message is loud and clear: whether we are male or female, old or young, unemployed, employee or employer, there are no advantages and no barriers when it comes to prophecy.

My wife Gill and I have four kids, and over the years we have woken them for many things: school, early

morning flights, work. With each child the response has
been different. Joshua is the most laid-back. Recently we
were sailing together, and in the middle of the night the
smoke alarm went off in our cabin. Does Josh wake up and
check the boat for fire? No way: he reaches from his bed
and, half asleep, takes the smoke alarm down, removes the
battery, and goes back to sleep within seconds! When Josh
was much younger, sometimes we would have to tickle
him to make sure he was properly awake. Our other son
Joel is just the opposite. The moment we called him to get
up he'd be awake and alert. If he'd been on the boat that
day he would have been wide awake, seeking out why the
alarm had gone off.

The fact is, we're all different; we all need different
things to wake us from our slumber and make us alert to
what is going on around us – but we all need waking at
some point!

I believe there is a wake-up call sounding in the
deepest recesses of the church. I believe God's voice is
calling out to us, 'Wake up, my people!' I believe the Holy
Spirit wants to shake us from our slumber and wipe the
sleep from our eyes so that we can see his work among us.
And that work very definitely, very importantly and very
strategically includes an increase in prophecy, not just in
our churches but out in the world, in our workplaces, our
communities, our schools and our government.

What is prophecy?

If I asked you 'What is prophecy?' what would you say
to me?

You might think about someone who foretells the future.
You might even conjure up images of the Old Testament
prophets, such as Elijah or Jeremiah, with their strange
lifestyles. You might recall how such prophets brought

warnings to God's people and called them to repentance, or spoke to religious and political leaders about what God expected and the consequences of disobedience. These are, of course, all perfectly valid ideas about prophets and prophecy. But there is far more than this. In the New Testament in particular, prophecy is painted with a much broader brush – and more significantly, it's a picture that we can more readily relate to and learn from.

To help unlock our faith and our thinking let's take a look at the Bible's use of the word 'prophecy'.

1. Prophecy occurs frequently in Scripture

- The word 'prophet' or 'prophets' appears 466 times.
- Other words like 'prophecy', 'prophesies' and 'prophetic' appear 163 times.

To put that in perspective, appearances of all the words related to teaching amount to around half that number. 'Preach' and 'preaching' occur only 120 times, while the words we'd expect to feature heavily, such as 'faith', 'belief' and 'believe', only total 487 appearances. I'm not suggesting that numbers equal importance. My point is that prophecy is an extremely strong thread throughout Scripture. Therefore, shouldn't we be taking it seriously?

2. The Hebrew words

The Old Testament prophet was called *ish elohim* or 'man of God'. That is, first and foremost, the prophet was seen as someone who was close to God. Prophets stood in a special relationship to God in a way that the ordinary Israelite did not. They could hear what God was saying, live it out and pass it on.

The Old Testament had two other words to describe the prophet:

- *Roeh*: 'seer' in English – someone who saw what was spiritually and physically hidden.
- *Hozeh*: a visionary – someone who could see what did not yet exist.

These words were gradually overtaken by the Hebrew word *nabi*, which means 'prophet' but has connotations of bubbling forth like a fountain.

A prophet was one who saw and then announced, or poured forth, the declarations of God. That could be a present but hidden truth or a prediction of something yet to happen. One scholar, Locke, says it encompassed three things:

1. Prediction
2. Singing by the spirit
3. Understanding and explaining the mysterious hidden sense of Scripture

3. *The Greek words*

In the New Testament we get a broader sense of the nature and application of prophecy. According to *Vine's Dictionary*, the Greek word for prophet – *prophetes* – means someone who speaks forth or openly, and prophecy – *propheteia* – means speaking forth the mind and counsel of God, declaring that which cannot be known by human or natural means.

To summarise both the Old and New Testaments, prophecy can be about

- Forthtelling: declaring who God is and what he has done; declaring his nature and attributes

- Foretelling: predicting future events
- Unlocking or interpreting the hidden sense of truth – including Scripture
- Inspired singing

With all this in mind, I like to think of prophecy like this:

> *The Spirit of God revealing something to an individual, which is then communicated to others, usually verbally, but also by music, visual arts and drama.*

What I'd like to do at this point is unpack some of the biblical attributes of prophecy, using practical, contemporary examples.

Forthtelling

One of the key dimensions of the prophetic is forthtelling: declaring who God is. Scripture itself is in many ways the best example of forthtelling. Many psalms resonate with this kind of prophetic activity:

> O LORD, our Lord, how majestic is your name in all the earth! You have set your glory above the heavens. From the lips of children and infants you have ordained praise because of your enemies, to silence the foe and the avenger. (Ps. 8:1–2)

> The LORD reigns for ever; he has established his throne for judgment. He will judge the world in righteousness; he will govern the peoples with justice. The LORD is a refuge for the oppressed, a stronghold in times of trouble. Those who know your name will trust in you, for you, LORD, have never forsaken those who seek you. (Ps. 9:7)

Reading scriptures such as these, particularly in a gathering, can encourage, comfort and build up the Body of Christ as their prophetic nature does its job. Equally, reading these scriptures aloud in your own company can build your faith and encourage you in your walk with God.

Taking our lead from the psalmists, we can see that it's perfectly acceptable for you and me to declare who God is in our own words.

If this seems a little daunting, however, try this little exercise:

- Take the initial letter of your first name and then the initial letter of your surname
- Take two minutes to write down attributes of God that begin with those two letters
- Take another two minutes to put them into a sentence which will declare who God is. Now read them out!

For example:

D – divine, dangerous, deliberate, demonstrable, dynamic, dominion, decisive.

R – redemption, redeemer, real, rock, right, rounded.

Forthtell:

'I believe in **redemption** – by a **deliberate**, **dynamic**, **real**, **demonstrable** and **divine Redeemer**. God is the **Rock**. He is **decisive**, **dangerous**, **right** and in a unique way a **rounded** role model.'

Another example:

J – joyful, joy, joker, just, Jewish, justified, Jehovah, judge, jester, Judah.

O – organised, ordained, ordinary, opportunity, outward looking, Oh so sweet.

Forthtell:
'**Joyful Jehovah** over all, you are **justified** in all things old and new. You were **oppressed** by all and rejected. We lift your name, **Jehovah**, above all. Hallowed be your name, **Oh so sweet** loving God. Creator of all, bringer of life, you are a **just judge** and **opportunity**-seeker. Over to you, Lion of **Judah**.'

Why not have a go for yourself, while the idea is still fresh in your mind?

Take the initial letters of your first name and surname and write them on the lines below. Now write all the attributes of God you can think of in two minutes:

_____

_____

_____

Now, using those words you've chosen, write a simple sentence to forthtell who God is:

_____

_____

_____

_____

Foretelling

Scripture is pregnant with more than six hundred prophetic promises. Many have yet to be fulfilled, but a good number come to fruition within the pages of Scripture with chilling accuracy:

> After we had been there a number of days, a prophet named Agabus came down from Judea. Coming over to us, he took Paul's belt, tied his own hands and feet with it and said, 'The Holy Spirit says, "In this way the Jews of Jerusalem will bind the owner of this belt and will hand him over to the Gentiles."' (Acts 21:10–11)

While such prophetic accuracy seems remarkable, it's not something limited to the pages of the Bible. Twenty-five years ago my own church, Basingstoke Community Church, started its own school. As you can imagine, starting a school, especially a Christian school, is not without its difficulties. During a night of prayer, one of our members warned us that we would have battles ahead with the local council and with financial difficulties, but that God would be faithful and see us through.

Sure enough, we encountered both of these before we finally achieved our goal. Admittedly, that word was very simple, but it was also very accurate. More importantly, it prepared us for the long haul, so that when we hit those foretold barriers we never once thought of wimping out. That prophecy gave us the confidence to call the church to times of prayer and to ask God to give us the wisdom to win those battles.

Inspired singing

> David, together with the commanders of the army, set apart some of the sons of Asaph, Heman and Jeduthun for the

ministry of prophesying, accompanied by harps, lyres and
cymbals. (1 Chr. 25:1)

While I was gathering my thoughts to write this chapter,
a woman in my church, Jane Cuff, began to sing the
following lines to a beautiful melody in the Sunday church
gathering:

Surrender, surrender, surrender
your heart to me.
Bow down, bow down, bow down
onto your knees.
Believe me, receive me, I love you.
Now be set free.

Soon after her singing, one or two other prophetic contributions were shared, each along the lines of surrender
to God. Moved by what he had heard, and by what the
Holy Sprit was doing within the congregation, one of the
leaders led us all into surrendering our past, our present
and our future to God. Though it was brought by people,
in reality this was God's gentle invitation to our church.
Equally, however, without Jane's obedience in singing that
Spirit-inspired song we would not have engaged with and
responded to God in that way.

A couple of days later, I asked Jane to explain the process
by which she had reached the point of taking the plunge
in a fairly large setting and singing that song. This is how
she told it:

I came downstairs Sunday morning to have breakfast
before church. As I sat down, I sensed the need to skip
breakfast and instead went back upstairs to clean my teeth.
As I stood in the bathroom, I found myself singing the first
line of a song over and over.

When I arrived at church, I spoke to the worship leader, telling her that I thought I had an inspired song, which I sang to her. To my encouragement, she indicated that she felt this was indeed something for the whole congregation and told me that she thought I would know the right time to sing it. During the service, someone shared a testimony, after which I sensed a gentle urging – I knew it was time. I was nervous, so the words actually helped me. I got the first line and the tune straightaway at home, and I got the third line on the way to church.

Notice the spirit in which Jane operated. First, she responded to the simplest nudge to skip breakfast. Notice too the fact that she didn't have all the content straightaway. I love the way she shared the song with the worship leader first. She didn't have to do that, and the Bible doesn't specifically suggest that she should, but even though she came with a strong contribution she was still prepared to have others take part in evaluating its appropriateness for the day (something we will look at in chapter 5).

I have seen and experienced inspired singing in many settings and in many different cultures. Sometimes when a song is being sung corporately it can feel as though it engages with what God is stirring in the congregation for that day. What I am describing is a familiar song or hymn which suddenly shifts to a different level as the Holy Spirit begins to work in the hearts and minds of those singing.

Another example is when someone sings out a short, simple song. This is then picked up by the congregation until everyone is singing it. I have witnessed this a number of times, when members of the congregation caught the melody and then began to add words of their own. I remember one evening when the song was sung over and over, by nearly everyone present, each time with fresh inspired words.

Summary

- Scripture tells us prophecy is for everyone, not just a gifted few
- Prophecy changes the life of the speaker, not just the hearer
- We live in a promised, prophecy-filled age
- Prophets come from all walks of life
- Prophecy is for every dimension of life: church, work, education, government
- We live in a God-given prophetic age
- Prophecy is multifaceted: forthtelling; foretelling, inspired singing, etc.

2

Who? What? When? Where?

I said in the last chapter that we live in a 'God-guaranteed prophetic age'. But the thing about a guarantee is that it is useless unless the holder applies its promise. *We are holders of a guarantee* from God that we live in a prophetic age – so let's apply that promise.

Paul understood that the promise of prophecy starts with us, all of us – and that includes you and me. There's no better indication of this than Paul's letter to the Corinthians, where he writes

> Eagerly desire the greater gifts. (1 Cor. 12:31)
> Eagerly desire spiritual gifts, especially the gift of prophecy. (1 Cor. 14:1)
> Try to excel in gifts that build up the church. (1 Cor. 14:12)
> All of these must be done for the strengthening of the church. (1 Cor. 14:26)
> Be eager to prophesy. (1 Cor. 14:39)

In the original Greek, these verses are imperatives – ongoing commands. Therefore, as Paul encourages us, we are to seek God for all manner of gifts – especially prophecy. And we're to desire them eagerly: it's a compelling command. What's more, sandwiched between Paul's double call to eagerly seek the gift of prophecy in 1 Corinthians 12 and 14 is his famous chapter on love. I'm sure Paul does this to emphasise that if you want to act out love, you should seek God with energy, commitment and persistence until you have these gifts, because they are for the benefit of others.

This is painting a very different picture to that we normally experience in evangelical and charismatic circles, where by and large the default attitude is, 'I'll bring something if God gives it to me.' Paul is saying the polar opposite. The shoe is on the other foot: it's our responsibility to make a conscious choice to seek God with zeal until we have something from heaven.

Paul's passion in these passages is quite striking. He is appealing to a Corinthian church that has become selfish and self-seeking, both physically and spiritually, to have an active passion for seeking spiritual gifts for the good of others. That's love in action.

The challenge for us is to consider how our lives line up with these commands:

- Do we actively, regularly and consistently ask and look for spiritual gifts – especially prophecy?

- What difference would it make to ourselves and others if we did?

As we start to engage with these gifts, we have another amazing promise:

From him [Christ] the whole body, joined and held together by every supporting ligament, grows and builds itself up in love, as each part does its work. (Eph. 4:16)

As we take our responsibility seriously, as we start to seek God and bring these gifts into the Body of Christ, so the church builds itself up. We become the Body of Christ, the community of Christ, the presence of Christ; for our families, for our communities, for our schools and colleges and for our places of work.

And please don't let this pass you by: *The church builds itself.*

No one else has to try to build it. How many times have you heard questions like this: '*How can we* see our church grow? *How can we* be more relevant to the community around us?' Well the truth is, 'we' can't – not in our own strength and through our own initiatives. Church leaders can't build churches, and neither can church programmes. What builds the church is our eagerness to seek God and the gifts of the Holy Spirit. If you're weary from trying to build your church, please let this promise liberate you.

Four areas of prophetic activity

In Scripture we see a variety of areas where the prophetic gift is expressed. I don't want to pretend these are some kind of theologically watertight definitions, but they may help to clear up some areas of confusion.

1. One-off, Spirit-led utterances
The book of Numbers records an occasion when Moses is speaking to the people of Israel. As he addresses them, God puts his Spirit on seventy elders.

> When the Spirit rested on them, they prophesied, but they did not do so again. (Num. 11:25)

These leaders had a moment in time, a one-off encounter with God's Spirit that enabled them to prophesy, which, as we know, never happened again.

There is also a fascinating story in 1 Samuel, where Saul's men, intent on capturing the fugitive David, go to a town called Naioth but end up 'captives' of God's Spirit.

> When they saw a group of prophets prophesying, with
> Samuel standing there as their leader, the Spirit of God
> came upon Saul's men and they also prophesied. Saul was
> told about it, and he sent more men, and they prophesied
> too. Saul sent men a third time, and they also prophesied.
> (1 Sam. 19:20–21)

Finally, hacked off by the failure of his men, Saul himself
goes to Naioth in search of David. He too, however,
succumbs to the Holy Spirit and ends up prophesying in
the presence of Samuel. But again, as far as we know, this
appears to be a unique event and not a permanent gift of
prophecy.

In chapter 1 we looked at Paul's statement that we
can all prophesy one by one. And in terms of declaring
who God is, I believe anyone can do that at any time. But
there are other times when more substantial words from
God can be brought by everyone present. I've personally
known this to happen, but it's rare. In twenty-five years
in Basingstoke Community Church, I've probably
witnessed this only five or six times. But they were of
course significant times.

It seems to work at another level too. I have found that
when I'm around someone with a more developed gift
than mine, it's as if something of it rubs off on me. I recall
travelling to India with a gifted evangelist friend of mine,
Vic Gledhill. Without any effort or special trying on my
part I found that during the entire trip I was engaging in
a level of evangelism that I would never normally do. On
another occasion, I travelled with John Paul Jackson, who
is a very gifted prophetic friend and one of the foremost
authorities on dreams and their interpretation. I saw
visions and had supernatural insights that I had never
had before, and have not experienced in the same way
since. In both cases, I can only assume it was the Spirit of

God and the extent of the gifting within these individuals that opened up possibilities for me.

2. Occasional use of the gift of prophecy

More common than one-off, unique moments of prophetic utterance are those cases in which people experience a prophetic gifting, but only occasionally, maybe once or twice a year. It's not a rule, but more often than not, this kind of gift will be something that encourages or comforts. For such people, prophecy is not a dominant part of their God-given gifts, but something they can draw on from time to time. My own wife, Gill, is a good example of this. From time to time I've known her impart prophetic words, often during prayer meetings. It's as if her prophetic side remains dormant, waiting for the most opportune time to awake.

3. Regular use of the gift of prophecy

For some people, prophecy is an everyday part of their spiritual make-up. They regularly exercise their gift not only in church meetings but also in their community or place of work. Usually this prophetic gift will take the form that we see in 1 Corinthians 14, bringing edification, exhortation and comfort. Judging by my experience, I would estimate that in most charismatic congregations between 5 and 10 per cent of the people will be acting prophetically on a regular basis. Our challenge is to seek these people out and release them so that they can bless our congregations and communities in the following ways:

- Inputting direction into meetings
- Bringing words of knowledge to individuals and the church

- Releasing the congregation into faith and worship
- Building up and encouraging the community of faith
- Bringing words into the workplace and the community

Such people are not necessarily limited to the above ways of operating, and may well also bring warnings, predictive words or strategic direction.

You may recall the story of Jane's inspired song recounted in chapter 1. She is typical of someone who regularly exercises the gift of prophecy, frequently bringing prophetic words during our meetings.

I think there is a biblical principle at work here. If we work faithfully with what we have, God will often give us more. It's rather like the Parable of the Talents (Mt. 25:14–30): the servant with two talents puts them to work and gains two more, and the man with five talents is likewise faithful in using what he has been given. Equally, a buried talent (or gift) is a wasted talent, and God is not slow to take away that which is being wasted. But the message of the parable is one of promise, not of judgement. We are left in no doubt that God will bless, enlarge and extend what we have, if only we have the eagerness to put it to work.

4. The Ephesians 4 ministry of the prophet
The examples of prophetic gifting we have considered so far can be likened to a spiritual gift given by God to individuals at a particular point in time in order to edify others. However, I believe that Ephesians 4 describes a unique role: here, it's not just that a person is given the gift of prophecy, but in some special way the prophet *is the gift of God*, wrapped in human flesh and given to equip others.

> It was he [Jesus] who gave some to be apostles, some to be prophets, ... to prepare God's people for works of service, so that the body of Christ may be built up. (Eph. 4:11–12)

To put it another way, the gift of prophecy is something that is given by God to an individual and then released or delivered to a person or group. *The prophet described in Ephesians 4 is a gifted person whose very presence equips others.*

So these are gifted people, given and appointed by Jesus in the church. They are not just people who prophesy regularly! It is part of their whole life and they are constantly doing it. They are likely to see foundations and to bring direction at a strategic level. The parameters of this kind of prophet are different to those of the gift of prophecy. These people have a job not just to bring prophetic words, but to equip others, bringing direction and vision to the church. Their role typically includes:

- Working with apostles as the foundation blocks of the church, bringing strategy, direction and vision
- Seeing, with apostles, what is right and wrong in church structure
- Equipping the church to be prophetic
- Recognising the giftings of others and being instrumental in their affirmation and release
- Preaching the Word

These prophets can be local, i.e. working primarily in one geographical area. However, it's more common for them to be itinerant, travelling to work with a range of churches and communities nationally, or quite possibly internationally.

How can we tell which kind of prophet we have?

I think the first three types of prophet, those who bring a gift or word of prophecy either on a unique occasion, from time to time or more regularly, are fairly self-evident.

The Ephesians 4 prophet, however, is someone entirely different, and not necessarily as easy to distinguish. As a helpful starting point, therefore, I'd like to suggest five attributes to look out for.

Attribute 1: Ephesians 4 prophets bring success

Success is a biblical word. Our success as a generation of churches in fulfilling God's call is intertwined with the ministry of the prophet. How can I say that confidently? The second book of Chronicles puts it like this:

> Have faith in the Lord your God and you will be upheld; have faith in his prophets and you will be successful. (2 Chr. 20:20)

Equally, Ezra 6:

> So the elders of the Jews continued to build and prosper under the preaching of Haggai the prophet and Zechariah. (Ezra 6:14)

The children of Israel fought with success because of the prophet. They built with success because of the preaching of the prophets. Success and prosperity in this biblical context do not mean riches; they simply mean knowing how to fight or build in God's ways with God's method for that moment.

Success for our congregations, for our cell groups, for our towns, for our particular church stream or denomination, for our workplace, even for our nation, is inextricably tied up with the type of prophet we encounter in Ephesians 4.

The prophets will bring strategy. And strategy gives us direction, a vision, a way ahead, as well as the steps necessary to get us there. One friend of mine put it like this:

> The prophet is up a tree, looking ahead, looking above the detail, getting the overview and essentially getting the direction. The apostle takes that information and applies it on the ground with the people, mobilises the people to take the journey, and gives them blueprints for how to tackle each step along the way.

If they are responsible under God for bringing success, sooner or later they will have a track record that proves this.

One of my friends, Andrew Shepherd, is particularly gifted in this way. I recall being with him at a dinner hosted by the national leadership of a large charity. Within minutes of the discussions starting, Andrew was at the heart of key issues relating to the organisation's growth, the strategy for the next twenty years and its leaders' desire to trust God for the growth of the charity. Within an hour, Andrew had seen a strategy and produced a cascade of tactical, practical applications to help the charity move forward.

Attribute 2: *Ephesians 4 prophets call us to seek God*

In 2 Chronicles 26, we see Uzziah seeking God during the days of Zechariah, who instructed him in the fear of God. The king sought God because the prophet instilled such an atmosphere within the royal court. In the Old Testament it's fascinating to trace the correlation between historic events and the relationship between the king and the prophet of the day. Kings regularly turned away from God when the prophetic influence faded or was unclear. There should be a violent urge in prophetic men and women to seek God and hear him above all else. And such urgency should spill over to apostles, leaders, congregations, cells and families.

In Amos 3 we read:

> Surely the Sovereign LORD does nothing without revealing his plan to his servants the prophets. (Amos 3:7)

That's a sobering truth. If we're doing a lot, but no one is hearing anything from God, we need to question whether God wants us to be doing this. Equally, we won't be hearing if we are too busy doing instead of stopping and listening! The prophet has a responsibility to hear, and also to encourage the church to seek God. If the prophet is not fulfilling this responsibility, the church is unlikely to hear God's plans. In such circumstances, we have to conclude that what we end up doing as churches is often not built in the way that God intends.

John Denning has for years been a prophetic voice in our group of churches, urging the leaders to call the people together to pray. John has become discouraged from time to time because leaders can seem uninterested, with the result that the people in those churches have drifted away from times of corporate prayer. But a group of us have encouraged John to keep at it, to keep raising the issue and to keep us alert to the need to press in to prayer.

I firmly believe that in our churches as a whole, corporate prayer has taken a knocking. We get unique moments such as Rob Parsons' initiative *Bringing Home the Prodigals*, in which over three years nearly 50,000 people have laid the names of prodigals at the foot of the cross. And as I write, we're looking forward to days of envisioning and commissioning prayer for the workplace, to be run by Care for the Family. But such events are exceptions to the rule.

As I write this chapter, Israel is at war with Lebanon. What saddens me is that I haven't seen or heard of any churches having corporate prayer events for these tragic events. In the last few years, I've witnessed little corporate prayer for the nation and for our towns or cities. In our own church, in the last few years we have come together to pray for our buildings and the school we run, but we haven't often engaged in corporate prayer for the nation, which provides the strategic framework into which these tactical issues fit. Again, I'm sure there are those of you reading this who know that such prayer does go on, but my point is that it is far too rare to enable the prophetic to be released into these urgent issues.

It's time for the prophetic voices to encourage us to pray. To stop being so introspective, to stop our navel-gazing and to think beyond our congregations, to love beyond ourselves and to stop keeping God to ourselves.

Attribute 3: *Ephesians 4 prophets are engaged in building the church*

I do not mean that the prophet gets involved in church bricks and mortar. Nor do I mean that the prophet builds the church in the sense of programmes or functions. What I mean is this: Jesus said, 'I will build my church' (Mt. 16:18). But it's the Ephesians 4 prophet who, along with the apostles, provides the foundation for church growth. So we see that

> From him [Jesus] the whole body … grows and builds itself
> up in love, as each part does its work. (Eph. 4:16)

The prophet prepares the people for works of service. That same prophetic gift provides strategy, direction and success, as the prophet speaks what he or she perceives God's plans to be, helping individuals, churches, families and even businesses to line up with the will of God. This prophet has the ability to see and convey direction to the entire Body of Christ and (as we shall see) to the world outside.

David Devenish of New Frontiers is a prophet who is able to equip the church to build. Working with Terry Virgo and David Holden, who have apostolic gifting, David is a consistent source of encouragement and motivation to others to get church-planting. David and some of his prophetic colleagues seek God for direction, strategy and guidance for application and bring it with authority into New Frontiers and indeed other church streams.

Attribute 4: Ephesians 4 prophets equip others to be prophetic

John Denning and I have worked together in the prophetic ministry for over thirty years. We have travelled tens of thousands of miles together. John and his wife Marilyn have trained and discipled over one hundred prophetic individuals.

In our six churches in Basingstoke, there are probably in the region of forty people with recognised and trained gifting in prophecy. We train them usually for two years at a time, with quarterly plenary sessions, followed by monthly cell group activity where we get individuals working on exercises to develop their prophetic skills. These evenings provide feedback, correction and encouragement. That's what I mean by equipping.

Attribute 5: *Ephesians 4 prophets see, affirm and release gifting in others*

It's not uncommon today to see 80 per cent or more of a congregation unsure of their gifts and not functioning fully in them. One of the key roles of an Ephesians 4-style prophet is to release that uncertain 80 per cent to fulfil the role and gifting God has set aside for them.

A good example of this is another close friend of mine who travels extensively and who will often see gifting in individuals. The way this works for him is usually in the form of images or symbols that he sees in his mind's eye. For example, if he sees the image of a trowel he will usually associate this with an apostolic gift. A pair of praying hands will indicate an intercessory gift. A shepherd's crook will denote a pastoral gift. The Bible or books will clue him in to a teaching gift, and so on.

Please don't take this to mean that these are fool-proof symbols that have universal application. They are merely examples to make the point. The truth is, God speaks to us all in different ways, and we must be open to this and learn the language God uses to communicate to us.

What's important is to recognise that through such Ephesians 4-type prophets, gifting is seen and affirmed and released to benefit the Body of Christ.

Getting the right perspective

God does not want us to have an inflated view of gifts and ministries; neither does he want us to downgrade or to devalue what he regards highly. In the mind and purposes of God the prophetic realm has tremendous significance.

Of the 39 books in the Old Testament, 34 were written, recorded or dictated by prophets. At my most mischievous,

I love to tell Bible teachers that. Even more, I love to remind the teachers that a vast amount of theology came from the prophets.

We are told clearly that the church is 'built on the foundation of the apostles and prophets, with Christ Jesus himself as the chief cornerstone' (Eph. 2:20). That's not flattery or theological comment, it's a structural necessity. The church cannot be built as God wants it to be without the foundation of apostles and prophets.

One summary of the Bible is that the Old Testament describes the dealings of God with his chosen people through priests, kings and *prophets*, while the New Testament describes his dealings with his royal priestly people through the apostles and *prophets*. In Old and New Testament the prophet's role was pivotal in the dealings of God with his creation and his chosen people. Crucially, the prophet's role has always been pivotal in God achieving his purposes on earth.

I believe God has said to the charismatic and evangelical church that just as we have seen the apostolic ministry birthed and developing in the last decade, so we shall see the growth of the prophetic ministry and its increasing release in this.

My own belief is that this season, early in the twenty-first century, will see a dramatic, wider release of the full manifestation of the gifts of the Spirit as the prophets do their work with fresh anointing and increasing ability.

New wineskins will unfold; new strategies will emerge in church planting, church building, prayer, evangelism and mobilisation, as the prophets come into their place of responsibility. This will not be just for the few but for the many – even for you and me.

Summary

- We are all called to eagerly desire the gifts of the Spirit
- Our gifts are foundational to building the church
- There are four areas of prophetic activity:
    1. *One-off, Spirit-led utterances*
    2. *Occasional use of the gift of prophecy*
    3. *Regular use of the gift of prophecy*
    4. *The Ephesians 4 ministry of the prophet*

- There are five attributes of an Ephesians 4 prophet:
    1. *Ephesians 4 prophets bring success*
    2. *Ephesians 4 prophets call us to seek God*
    3. *Ephesians 4 prophets are engaged in building the church*
    4. *Ephesians 4 prophets equip others to be prophetic*
    5. *Ephesians 4 prophets see, affirm and release gifting in others*

- The prophet is pivotal in God achieving his purposes on earth

3

How Does God Speak?

God is love (1 Jn. 4:16). And love needs to be communicated.

God loves us and he desires that the loved ones hear his voice. But unfortunately it would seem that far too often God is more willing to speak than we are keen to listen.

> God does speak – now one way, now another – though man may not perceive it. (Job 33:14)

Think of the passage we have already discussed in 1 Corinthians 14. Remember the statement, 'You can all prophesy one by one'? Well, I believe that's God's way of saying that he will speak to everyone and give us something to say. In fact, we should have total confidence that God will speak.

> For there is nothing hidden that will not be disclosed, and nothing concealed that will not be known or brought out into the open. Therefore consider carefully how you listen. (Lk. 8:17–18)

Though the book of Proverbs says that 'it is the glory of God to conceal a matter' (Prov. 25:2), it is not the heart of God to hide those things from those who seek them earnestly. God loves us to press in and discover the hidden things. This is a 'game' of hide-and-seek with a promise. As Jesus himself said,

> Seek and you will find. (Mt. 7:7)

Keep looking: you will discover. Keep asking: you will get your answer. Keep knocking: the door will be opened.

Ways in which God speaks

In Scripture we are treated to a kaleidoscope of different ways in which God speaks to his people and the world at large. Hebrews tells us that God spoke through the prophets 'at many times and in various ways' (Heb. 1:1). He is a God of infinite variety, and the way he chooses to speak reflects that.

Before the Fall, communication with God was direct and relaxed, taking place on a walk in the cool of the day (Gen. 3:8). But once the communications lines had been disrupted by a major fault – sin – things became a little more tricky.

God speaks to Abraham, the father of our faith, through visions and dreams and via angels (Gen. 12 – 25).

Moses hears a burning bush talk (Ex. 3).

Samuel hears a voice that keeps waking him up (1 Sam. 3).

Ezekiel has all kinds of strange experiences (Ezek. 1:15–21, 3:1, 5:1–4).

Daniel has dreams and visions and, along with King Belshazzar, even sees a detached finger writing on a plaster wall (Dan. 5).

Mary, Jesus' mother, has an angelic visitation (Lk. 1:26–28).

Wise men follow celestial bodies (Mt. 2).

The apostle Paul is enveloped in brilliant light and hears the voice of Jesus (Acts 9).

Peter sees a sheet full of food (Acts 10:11–12).

And John gets the trip of a lifetime! (Rev. 4).

Though all these experiences are God-given, it has to be said that there is some weird and wonderful stuff going on here. And I'd wager that with the exception of dreams, these aren't common, everyday experiences for most of us.

What's more, in listing these events, I have made three important omissions. Did you spot them?

The three most common ways God speaks to us are missing:

- The written Word of God
- Prayer
- The created order

If we are looking to move into the prophetic, we shouldn't necessarily be expecting God to move in mysterious ways, especially if we have neglected the obvious. In fact, understanding that more often than not God uses the ordinary and not the extraordinary can be a true release for us when we are seeking what he wants to say to his church and the world.

1. *The written Word of God*

God has spoken. And God still speaks to us through the Bible. We are truly blessed that we have the Scriptures readily available and can routinely seek to allow God's Word to impact our lives. As the psalmist wrote,

> Your word is a lamp to my feet and a light for my path (Ps. 119:105).

Even within Scripture itself we have the example of Daniel, who weighed what he was seeing and hearing against the written words of the prophet Jeremiah. I find this particularly potent, given that the revelations given to Daniel were incomparable with anything I've witnessed, and yet he still naturally and instinctively measured them against what God had already said.

'All Scripture is God-breathed' (2 Tim. 3:16). Little wonder, then, that keeping our minds and spirits regularly engaged with Scripture feeds us with keys, nuggets and impressions that will often form the basis of a prophetic word.

2. Prayer

Jesus is the example *par excellence* of using prayer to hear the Father, in order to do what God wants done and to speak out what God wants people to hear. He would often go to lonely places, away from domesticity and busyness and into the natural world of mountains and deserts, in order to pray. Prayer, together with his rich knowledge of the Word of God, was the source of Jesus' revelation. The same is true of Abraham, Elijah, Isaiah, Jeremiah and Habakkuk. To get words from God we need to spend time with God, and there simply is no shortcut.

3. Nature, creation and everyday objects

God spoke through the natural world to both Old and New Testament prophets. As you read Scripture you will see hundreds of examples of God speaking as the prophets see everyday objects and created things. Jeremiah is sent by God to the potter's house, where he sees a common commercial artistic process under way. As he watches the potter on the wheel, he sees a slip of the finger. The clay is misshapen, and on a whim, it seems, the potter chooses to make something else from the spinning clay. As Jeremiah watches this, maybe his heart rate quickens, maybe the sense of clarity dawns or maybe the hairs on his neck stand on end. However it worked for Jeremiah, he clearly now senses God giving him a word:

> O house of Israel, can I not do with you as this potter does? (Jer. 18:6)

See the process. A sense that God wants him at the potter's house and a minor moment on the wheel triggers the flow of God speaking. Mix that with his political awareness of the times and his understanding of Israel's spiritual condition, and somehow out of all that the word of prophecy comes.

For most of us, the written Word of God and the formation of pictures, words or images in our minds is how we will begin to see and hear God. It's as if the picture or image we see is an embryo. It's not yet fully formed, but all the potential is contained within it. And as we learn to let God clarify it, and allow our gifting to shape it, sooner or later we will give birth to a fully-formed prophecy.

Of course, this gives rise to the question of how we can apply such prophetic vision practically. To try to answer this, I asked some friends of mine to write down how they receive what might ultimately become a prophetic word or a revelation.

How do we receive prophetic words?

Mike Madden responds:

> In terms of receiving prophetic words, the basic process has not changed for me. I usually see a surprising picture, something that breaks into my consciousness. The process of giving the prophetic word, however, has changed considerably.

In the early days I would often sit in the meeting, sweating, worrying – Is it God? Is it me? – waiting for a confirming word from someone else before stepping out. I would give the word quickly, wanting to dump it on the poor unsuspecting congregation. Looking back, although I always tried to make sure I followed the guidance of Scripture that prophetic words should be encouraging, comforting, upbuilding, etc., I feel I was often harsh, proud, even superior. I tended to shout, and did not always talk tenderly to God's people.

Twenty-five years later the zeal, the passion and the desire to see God's love touch people have not changed, but I would like to think I am more compassionate. I no longer feel the need to prophesy for my benefit, but rather it is about serving God and serving the Body of Christ. Now, when I receive a picture, I take much more care to look deeply into what God has given me, taking care to consider it prayerfully. I am much more likely to share what God has said with other prophetic people and to look to God for confirmation of what I've seen or heard. I would like to think it is now more about him and less about me, more about seeing God's people enter into everything he wants for them.

John Denning writes in response to the same question:

In my early days, prophesying would usually come through impressions and pictures. Mostly these words and pictures would spring from my reading of the Scriptures, but not exclusively. Often I would become conscious of the Spirit speaking and showing me insights that had encouraging aspects relating to people's lives.

During the late 1960s, I began to experience what turned out to be prophetic dreams. Given my work at that time as a farmer, the dream content would often be agricultural or relate to my family. I discovered that God often uses our background, that which is familiar, to bring meaning into prophetic dreams.

It was at this time that I discovered that praise and intimacy of worship would inspire me in seeing and speaking prophetically. I also began to notice how often Jesus referred to 'listening' and 'considering', and I have sought to make this a reality in my own life. Learning to listen to God has become a very deep longing, not just a discipline but a yearning to know him.

The change that has taken place in me over the years is to understand the various kinds of prophetic gifting and to recognise the one into which I fit. I'm comfortable with who I am in God and no longer feel the pressure to be like others or seek the same gifts.

Phil Thomas says:

The majority of words I receive from the Lord come in the form of mental images. These tend to relate to areas of my personal experience. There is good scriptural precedent for God speaking through illustrations from daily life – things we know well. The book of Isaiah in particular teems with examples of the prophet calling to the people using illustrations from their daily lives – farming, nature, human relationships.

When I have received the 'picture', sometimes the meaning is obvious. But often I have to ask the Lord what the image means for the person(s) concerned. The interpretation of the picture for the particular situation then comes into my mind – though this process is difficult to put into words.

An example is probably the most useful way to express what I mean.

I had a picture of a marine pilot vessel alongside a supertanker, guiding it into and out of port. (I grew up in

Southampton, so illustrations from the sea and the marine environment feature commonly for me.) I clearly saw the pilot on the bridge of the tanker advising the captain and crew how to navigate the local waters. This word was for a church leader with an apostolic ministry who was seeking to change direction. I felt God say that his role was to be like that of the pilot – not leading churches himself, but coming alongside other church leaders to instruct, guide and encourage, so that they could find the way forward for their churches.

How I receive words has not changed much since I began moving in the prophetic. However, I do find that the words I receive are much 'sharper' if, when I know I will be called on to prophesy, the time is preceded by a period of fasting.

How do I hear from God?

Andy Shepherd tackles this question:

Obviously, I hear God speak to me through reading the Bible. But God isn't limited to his Word. Music, radio, films and jokes can all be a platform to hear from God. I often sense God's presence when I spend time in art galleries. I find it particularly helpful to be in God's creation. Regularly I try to get on the ocean or mountains. I find the atmosphere of reflection and wonder of being in big, unlimited environments very helpful for listening openly, without barriers or prejudice. This means planning, investing time to get there, and doing it.

Tip: find your place of 'solitude', wherever or whatever it might be to you. We are all different, and different environments work for different people. In this way, you can encounter God, be restored and refreshed, and be in a tender, receptive frame of mind.

I also find that I hear God in the form of a 'sense' or 'image' during times of worship or quiet reflection. I say 'sense' because it is probably awareness of a thought that immediately seems profound or relevant. It is important to emphasise that this 'sense' of God or thought is like the tiniest whisper, as light as a feather, that could easily be missed or dismissed (and it often is). Yet this delicate sensing or thought is durable and lasts.

Through these personal stories, I hope you will have noticed that there is no one single way in which God speaks to us. But there is a common thread: a scripture that comes alive, an image seen, a mental impression or an actual observation of something during the preceding hours or days.

The Old Testament prophet Jeremiah is a great example of this:

> The word of the LORD came to me: 'What do you see, Jeremiah?'
>
> 'I see the branch of an almond tree,' I replied.
>
> The LORD said to me, 'You have seen correctly, for I am watching to see that my word is fulfilled.'
>
> The word of the LORD came to me again: 'What do you see?'
>
> 'I see a boiling pot, tilting away from the north,' I answered.
>
> The LORD said to me, 'From the north disaster will be poured out on all who live in the land. I am about to summon all the peoples of the northern kingdoms,' declares the LORD. (Jer. 1:11–14)

You see the principle. An image triggers a response towards God, and then somehow or other a sense of what God is saying permeates through.

Let me illustrate this from a personal example.

I was asked by some close friends to seek God for a young lady in their church who was accepted into the Royal Marines Band Service. They were going to pray with her and ask God's blessing and direction for her. I was in the middle of a busy period, so the first thing I had to do was to get myself some quiet moments to pray and then ask God for something for this young woman. Almost immediately I saw a beautiful hand holding what looked like a very beautiful and tender green shoot, planting it in what was clearly a different place. As I kept looking and reflecting, the words 'tender shoot' came strongly to mind, followed by 'good intent', 'good purpose' and 'kindness' in relation to the hand. As I kept looking, the ground in which this shoot was being planted was full of unpleasant, old, rusty things such as tin cans, barbed wire and rotting weed matting. I knew the Scripture had an application concerning tender shoots, so I looked until I found Ezekiel 17:22–24. The word then came together as follows:

'This is what the Sovereign LORD says: "I myself will take a shoot from the very top of a cedar and plant it; I will break off a tender sprig from its topmost shoots and plant it on a high and lofty mountain. On the mountain heights of Israel I will plant it; it will produce branches and bear fruit and become a splendid cedar. Birds of every kind will nest in it; they will find shelter in the shade of its branches. All the trees of the field will know that I the LORD bring down the tall tree and make the low tree grow tall. I dry up the green tree and make the dry tree flourish. I the LORD have spoken, and I will do it."'

I see Anna like a plant or a shoot being picked carefully by the hand of God – a hand of intent and good purpose and a hand with kindness in it. The hand places her tender shoot into a very different soil – old bits of rusted metal

and barbed wire, old discarded materials, jagged bricks
and general rubbish lie below the surface. The plant seems
weak and vulnerable and incapable of flourishing in the
soil. But there is good life in this tender shoot and it will
prevail. What's more, the plant itself will be strengthened
by the process.

Actually, in time, whatever the outcome of this move, if
Anna will lean on God, he will see to it that she bears fruit,
her life becoming a shelter for others.

The process then, was as follows:

- Prayer – setting aside time to hear God and asking
  him specifically to speak
- Noting down the first images that came to mind
- Looking again at the images and seeing more
- Being aware of three or four key words that began
  to form a thread
- Finding the scripture that was calling for my
  attention
- Putting it together
- Taking it back to God and asking for clarity and
  affirmation

Summary

- God is love – and love desires to communicate
- God wants us to seek and discover what he has to
  say
- God speaks to us in all kinds of ways
- Typically God speaks to us through his Word, prayer
  and created things

4

Developing the Gift

There are a number of ingredients in learning to develop a prophetic gift. The first one is a practical principle, often called stewardship.

One of the most famous of the great stories Jesus told is the Parable of the Talents, and there are some striking things to discover in it.

You remember the story. The boss calls on his three servants before going on an overseas trip and entrusts his property to them. One servant is entrusted with five talents (the equivalent of hundreds of pounds), another with two talents and the third with just one. The servant who had received the five talents went at once and put his money to work and gained five more. So, also, the one with the two talents gained two more. But the man who had received one talent went off, dug a hole in the ground and hid his master's money.

After a while the boss returns and wants to settle accounts. Matthew then records the following:

> The man who had received the five talents brought the other five. 'Master,' he said, 'you entrusted me with five talents. See, I have gained five more.'
>
> His master replied, 'Well done, good and faithful servant! You have been faithful with a few things; I will put you in

charge of many things. Come and share your master's happiness!'

Then the man who had received the one talent came. 'Master,' he said, 'I knew that you are a hard man, harvesting where you have not sown and gathering where you have not scattered seed. So I was afraid and went out and hid your talent in the ground. See, here is what belongs to you.'

His master replied, 'You wicked, lazy servant! ... you should have put my money on deposit with the bankers, so that when I returned I would have received it back with interest. Take the talent from him and give it to the one who has the ten talents. For everyone who has will be given more, and he will have an abundance. Whoever does not have, even what he has will be taken from him.' (Mt. 25:20–29)

If you and I put to work what we have, we are rewarded with more. My responsibility, and your responsibility, is not how much we have been given, but what we do with it.

The person with one talent is like many in the church today who don't seek God for the gifts he has for them and don't put to work what they already have. Before too long then, even the little they thought they had gets taken away. It's lost to them and, just as importantly, the gift is lost to the people around them, who could have been the beneficiaries.

Burying our gift

I think a question that needs to be asked is this: Why do Christians with one talent bury it?

I believe that the three most common reasons are

- Fear
- Comparing ourselves with others

- Not knowing what God desires from us

1. Fear

Most people, when they first start to prophesy, get nervous: 'What if I'm wrong?' 'What if I dry up?' 'What if the leaders correct me?' 'Will people think, Oh no it's her again?'

Somehow, this fear needs to be dealt with. And the best way to deal with fear is to face it head-on.

If you struggle with nervousness, as I have done (and occasionally still do), find someone else with a prophetic gift and ask them to support you as you work out your own gifting. If you are concerned about whether or not you've heard from God, share your thoughts with someone you trust.

From time to time I have had the opportunity to speak prophetically in some rather large gatherings. To keep fear at bay, I make it a habit in such meetings to be around other prophetic people I trust, in order that we can share with one another the essence of what we feel God is saying before taking to a platform.

I love the fact that sometimes being fearful can be the very thing that brings you a big dose of practical wisdom.

Working together is not only a wise thing to do; it's an encouraging thing to do. Sometimes, on the cusp of wavering, I've looked across at those I trust, to be greeted with a big thumbs-up or an affirming 'Go for it!' We need to get away from thinking of prophets as maverick loners. Even Jesus drew people around him whom he could trust: a 'ministry' team, if you like. Indeed, when Jesus sent his disciples out, he sent them in teams. Time and time again the New Testament talks about 'prophets' in the plural or 'apostles and prophets' together as a team.

2. *Comparing ourselves with others*

Though it might not appear so at first, I believe that
comparing ourselves with others is far more insidious
than fear can ever be when it comes to robbing us of our
gifting.

I speak personally, because I have had the privilege
of working with men and women whose gifting, in my
perception at least, is way beyond mine. And the problem
with believing that is that when I'm in their presence it's
all too easy for me to bury what God has given me.

I'm a realist: I know that people cannot help but compare
what they have to offer with others' gifts – and that can
easily make us feel desperately insecure. What results is
an inner reluctance to share anything.

I think this problem is particularly acute for those who
are working with a fledgling gift. How easy it is for them to
compare themselves with, or try to be like, those who are
known within the church to be moving in the prophetic.

If you know you're struggling with comparing yourself
with others, let me try to help.

When you compare your contribution, do you feel as
though you've produced the scribble of a young child while
others have presented a masterpiece?

Well, let me tell you this. My children are now independent, intelligent and articulate adults. But that doesn't
mean that I don't still keep and treasure the very first
scribbles they made as children. In fact, they are of equal
worth to anything they give to me now. Why? Because they
are my children and I love them, and I value them, and
I know that for their age and at that stage in their lives,
they had given of their best. They hadn't buried their talent
just because it didn't match up to the masterpiece that is
the Sistine Chapel. What they had done was to bring me
their best, drawn with love. For years I carried one such

scribble with me all around the world because I treasured it so much.

> When they measure themselves by one another, and compare themselves with one another, they are without understanding. (2 Cor. 10:12)

Let me encourage you not to make comparison an excuse for burying the gift you carry, and instead to have a go with what you've got!

3. Not knowing what God desires from us

The Gospel writer Luke tells of Jesus recounting a story similar to the Parable of the Talents, recorded by Matthew (Lk. 19:11–27). What both these parables seem to indicate is a lack of understanding by the servant who is given the single talent (or mina, in the case of Luke's account) as to what his Lord desired from him. The other servants knew that they were expected to use what had been given to them, and they were blessed accordingly. But the servant with just the one talent shows a singular lack of awareness of his master's reason for giving him this gift.

Don't bury your gift. Your God has given it to you so that you can put it to good use.

If any of these reasons is preventing you from using your God-given gift, I encourage you to recognise that, pray about it, and seek out those whom you trust to encourage you. Put your gifts to work and steward them as best you can. Seek God for the times and places to exercise them and for the people God wants to speak to, and let them be an increasing blessing to others.

Development in a team

The second area of development is working together with other prophets or prophetically gifted people.

In several places in the Old Testament we come across groups of prophets working together. There seem to be such groups attached to the temple and in the royal courts. During David's reign these would have included those who were singers and instrumentalists. There were also schools of prophets. To clarify this, the term 'school' is not necessarily an educational or training environment but rather a collective noun, rather like a shoal of fish or a flock of birds. Having said that, in the three schools mentioned (Bethel, Jericho and Gilgal) there was clearly a measure of training and discipleship going on. In the days of Elijah and Elisha this seemed to consist of prophets encouraging each other in matters of faith and gifting. But they did practical things as well, such as building and manual work. From time to time a more senior prophet would send a trainee, e.g. Elisha sent someone to give a prophetic message to Naaman.

Interestingly, such schools were at their strongest during a time when the national faith was weak. Given the current climate, perhaps we need to take this on board.

The example that we considered earlier, of Saul's men prophesying, was in the context of a group of prophets prophesying. In 1 Samuel 10:10 the term 'procession of prophets' is used – like David's royal court, they processed with musical instruments (1 Sam. 10:5). Given that they were coming from Gilgal, it's reasonable to assume they were part of the school of prophets based there.

There was also a process of discipleship. The best known example would be that of Elijah and Elisha. Although less clear, a form of prophetic discipleship is also implied in the case of Elisha and Gehazi. There is also evidence that this was happening in Isaiah's time, and the New Testament prophet John the Baptist had a very visible group of disciples.

What all this background leads us to is a clear understanding that going it alone will not develop the prophetic gift as well as it could be developed within a team context.

We see a similar pattern in the New Testament. From Acts onwards, the plural word 'prophets' is used forty-five times, compared with only a couple of mentions of the singular 'prophet'. When Agabus comes down to Antioch, he is the only one whose name is mentioned, but he is part of a group of prophets (Acts 11:28). Scripture talks a number of times about the pairing of apostles and prophets. We also see teachers and prophets grouped together. Paul had prophetic individuals on his team, most notably Silas and, I assume, John Mark. The first letter to the Corinthians talks about prophets, in the plural, weighing the prophetic words of the other prophets in their groups.

I have the privilege of working with Rob Parsons and Jonathan Booth in Care for the Family. Rob has seen a number of prophetically gifted individuals join Care for the Family over the years. While Rob is clearly a world-class communicator, I see him as having a very clear prophetic gift. His gift has enabled him both formally and informally to train, mentor, encourage and sharpen many people in different ways. Rob will listen to recordings of events I do and take the time to give me feedback, confronting me in areas where he feels I am damaging or hindering the message for the hearers. I have learned so much from this process, and I am a better communicator because of it.

In the group of churches I belong to (Salt and Light) we have had a number of training events with hundreds of prophetically gifted individuals from our various churches taking part.

In Basingstoke we have had several prophetic development groups, the results of which have been very gratifying. There is also a process of formal and informal discipleship. We have several apostolic leaders who are travelling regularly and who take a mixture of experienced and inexperienced prophets with them. That is an amazing training and development process. Working in large auditoriums or small house groups, or visiting people in their workplaces or communities, offers a rich variety of opportunity, enabling the gift to be practised and adjusted with the invaluable input of experienced people.

One friend of mine, Dave Richards, regularly takes teams into Zimbabwe, Kenya and France, and all over the UK. He would say it is the exception not to have at least one prophetic person on a team, as he values the role of the prophet so highly. Dave is a great trainer and fantastic at developing people. In fact, in twenty years of working with him, I have never yet heard of anyone who hasn't valued the experience of being part of one of his teams.

I've often been involved in leading groups of prophetic people to seek God on behalf of others. The experienced and the less experienced work together on these teams. Words are carefully collated and are part of the debriefing process, so that all of us can take responsibility for what we bring, and all of us can learn. A similar experience takes place when we take a team into a house group. We always allow the cell groups to feed back how the different words have helped them, or not, as the case may be. In developing prophetic gifts it's important to learn how accurate or not words have been, and so to seek God together regarding how those words should be handled.

More formal discipleship also often takes place within the prophetic development group. Here there may be weekly or fortnightly accountability sessions. Written and practical assignments will be given, and the results marked. Other times a group of prophetic men and women will meet for cheese and wine, or maybe for a time of prayer and sharing together.

In all these means of development the important thing is plurality and relationship. Doing things together, encouraging and challenging each other – learning, and allowing the group to have positive input.

The key is this: *Don't go it alone.*

- Make yourself available for teams
- Be part of a training programme
- Find someone to mentor or disciple you
- Be a facilitator to enable other prophets to meet

Development with discipline

The moment a word like discipline is used there can be a negative response. It feels legal. It feels constricting. Understandably, the free spirit of the prophet can take umbrage at the thought.

Often people will come to a training programme or an event looking for techniques and quick fixes to achieve more potent prophecy. I'd love to tell you such things exist – but they don't.

Discipline and *application* are keys to better prophecy.

The two most obvious disciplines to develop are *prayer* and *reading the Word of God*. We mentioned these in the last chapter and we need to mention them again here.

The Word of God is the only foolproof source of revelation we have. The more we are steeped in it, the more it can influence, shape and mould our life and our words.

Prayer, too, is a must for people operating in the prophetic. One of my friends will often spend time – perhaps an hour or so – just resting with a notebook, giving that time to God. Another friend tries to carve out chunks of time in his week to get time alone with God.

Most of us can engage in prayer together if we choose to meet to do just that. When we do, let's make sure we give time to listen as well as to ask.

Even as I write this, I can hear some of you complaining that giving over such time to God is unrealistic. You've got tough jobs with long hours. You've got a house to run, kids to look after and endless other tasks to perform just to keep your head above water. Believe me, I do understand. But if we want to be serious about moving in the prophetic, we need to find time for prayer.

This is an area that I have found quite difficult. I have a fairly hectic business life with a reasonable amount of travel. For me, regular, small amounts of prayer are the norm, not hours waiting on God.

When I was baptised my dad gave me the scripture 'Pray without ceasing'. I have taken that to mean: pray regularly, whenever and wherever. So I will comfortably pray in a plane, a hotel, a lounge, or a shop in the town centre. It becomes a way of life and it's a way that I can manage. I will do that alone, or with others; it's the way prayer works for me.

Whatever your particular circumstances, when you shower, drive to work, sit with your coffee at lunchtime or do the dishes, how about developing a habit of prayer for a few minutes at a time can make a radical difference to your life and to the lives of others.

3 minutes of prayer, 5 times a day

= 105 minutes a week

= 91 hours a year

What a difference that would make!

Growing the seeds of prophecy

Most of us love instant results. We live in a 'now' culture, and that immediacy has infiltrated the church.

I suppose if there were a packet of seeds which could be planted today and harvested tomorrow, the inventor would be the richest man in the world, because every farmer or allotment holder would want them. But nature doesn't work that way, and neither does the Creator of the seed.

One of the ways this works out in practice is that God will more often than not give us seed, rather than harvest. Jesus taught us that the word of God is a seed. In the Parable of the Sower, Jesus describes the seed as the word of God. How big is a seed in relation to the plant it grows into? Tiny!

When preaching on this parable, I love to start by giving every person present a seed. It's fascinating to watch people trying to figure out what to do with it. Some slyly drop it on the floor, hoping no one sees them. Others put it in a page of their Bible. Still others pass it to their partner, while others just hold it in their hands, wondering if I will put them out of their misery at some point and explain why it is that I've given them a seed.

The point is simply made. Most of us don't know what to do with a physical seed when it is given to us unexpectedly. In nearly every case, it is discarded or thrown away and dies, its potential for life unrealised.

The same is true with revelation. It will often come in a seed so small that we can easily let it slip through our fingers or simply miss it altogether. Some of us may simply be unimpressed with the seed and discard it. Some try to express the seed in its current form and miss the fullness of revelation that God intended.

How can we nurture these seeds and at least give them a chance to germinate? Well, they need planting in a place where you can feed, water and nurture them.

One practical thing that helps me in this context is a small notebook which acts as a journal. It's effectively my seedbed, or cold frame, in which I plant the seeds of ideas or words. I then revisit them in prayer from time to time to bring them on. I write my prayers, my frustrations and my hopes. I also write down any verse, passage or question that impacts me.

- If I feel I am getting a little seed of revelation, I will write 'seed' by it
- If I feel I am getting some kind of prophetic word, I will write a big 'P' by it
- If I sense a particular message for preaching or teaching, I write a big 'M' by it
- If I am recording a dream, I write a big 'D' by it

By doing this, I find that when I go back through the book it's easy to see where God has spoken to me.

Developing through eagerness

There is always the danger in discussing an area like this that we can go in the opposite direction and try to develop these seeds in our own strength. However, when the gift and the calling are in place, I believe we have a responsibility to develop what we have to the maximum.

Someone once said that we become as small as our controlling desire or as great as our dominant aspiration. In this context, are we committed to the effort required to develop our gifts to the full?

What is my dominant aspiration? Can I truthfully say that to serve God I will develop this gift to my best ability? Remember, we are to be eager in seeking the gifts of God.

Our spiritual lifestyle should never be one of contentment with what we have. We shouldn't be looking for a short-term investment with big returns and early retirement. Rather we should be eager and active, determined, aspiring to do the very best we can.

We need to ask ourselves two challenging questions:

1. *Am I lazy with the gift?*

In Proverbs we read that 'the lazy man does not roast his game' (Prov. 12:27). This may seem like a strange verse to quote, but in fact it's very pertinent. I've had far too many prophecies served up to me over the years that are inedible because the prophet has been too lazy to 'roast' them! Instead of a feast, we get a corpse. What God desires to give the church is a banquet of prophecy – but he needs prophets willing to take the time to prepare and 'roast' the words so the church can be truly nourished.

2. *Do I pass the 'look' test?*

Look at the following list of activity from just one chapter (7) in the book of Daniel:

- He wrote down the substance of the dream (v. 1)
- In my vision at night I looked (v. 2)
- I watched (v. 4)
- I looked (v. 6)
- I looked (v. 7)
- I was thinking (v. 8)

- I looked (v. 9)
- I continued to watch … I kept looking (v. 11)
- I looked (v. 13)
- I asked (v. 16)
- I wanted to know (v. 19)
- I also wanted to know about (v. 20)
- I watched (v. 21)

Daniel is totally engaged with the vision he has been given. He doesn't just get the vision and think, 'Wow, that was amazing. Thanks, God.' Rather, he is completely immersed, continually asking, looking, thinking and looking again, not wanting to miss anything, making sure he gets things right.

Let's put it this way: how many of us would have simply forgotten the dream by the morning because we didn't write it down? How many of us would only have seen the four great beasts and missed the rest?

Daniel was a world-class prophet. He wasn't lazy, but kept pressing on until he got more in content, more in understanding and more in interpretation.

Back to our seeds. Sometimes God will give you something that's fast-growing. Sometimes you will have to store your seed away in the cold frame of your journal and look again, days, weeks, months or even years later.

Occasionally a picture may be fairly complete, in which case let's not go to the other extreme, trying to make a Rolls-Royce out of a Mini. It's more common, though, to be given the blueprints rather than the car. So let's encourage one another to develop an attitude that has faith to believe that God wants to reveal more, an attitude that looks for more, asks for more, prays for more, waits for more.

Summary

- We need to put our 'talent' to use
- Don't let fear, comparison or ignorance bury your gift
- The best prophecy can come via teamwork
- Prophecy takes discipline
- Prophecy is a seed that needs time to grow
- Don't be lazy, be engaged

5

Weighing and Being Weighed

In the previous chapter I made it clear that prophecy can be at its best when the prophet is part of a team. What I want to do now is take a look at one of the most important reasons for the prophet to be accountable to others – the weighing of prophecy.

One of the first and most important things to say is that allowing your prophetic words to be weighed is actually one of the most positive things you can do to enhance, enjoy and develop your prophetic gift.

One of the things that saddens me most is to see gifted, prophetic people who either will not submit their words or revelation to be weighed or, more commonly, simply have no one who is willing to take on this responsibility. I believe this is one of the enemy's greatest coups in relation to muzzling the prophetic or discouraging those who are gifted prophetically. Church leaders especially must learn to take on this responsibility and learn how to weigh prophecy in a way which builds and does not crush the prophetic gift.

Let's face up to some reality at the outset. It is a generalisation, but a reasonably accurate one, to state that most gifted prophetic people are prone to insecurity. I'm not sure why this is the case, only that this insecurity is a significant barrier to realising the prophetic in our churches.

I know what it's like to have someone tell you that the word you have brought is not from God. It's a crushing blow to your confidence, making you far less likely to bring something in the future, however sure you feel that God has spoken to you. Not only that, it's a cause of embarrassment. It's demeaning and it can affect your relationship with your church leadership.

Making it right when it's all gone wrong

I should make it clear that I'm not being naive. I've been around prophets and the church long enough to witness my fair share of words that have not been from God and the havoc they can wreak – and such things need to be dealt with seriously. My point is this: two wrongs can never make things all right.

I recall a friend of mine who was asked to preach in a huge church in Zimbabwe. As he prepared his talk, he sensed God giving him a message about waging war in line with the prophetic words given. The worship in the church that night was powerful, and he was going to stand up to preach at a time when the presence of God was strong. Right at that point, a young man came up to the microphone. My friend's heart sank. I remember him telling me that for some reason he just knew that they were about to be treated to something off the wall.

'There is sin in this church, and there are three areas,' the young man began.

My friend whispered to a team member, 'He'll go for sex, money and pride.'

Sure enough, the young man continued his prophecy and did indeed prophesy that there were sins in the church relating to sex, money and pride.

My friend was in a fix. How could he preach about waging war through the prophetic word when such an off-the-wall, untimely prophecy had just been given? To his relief, the pastor of the church took the microphone and said this:

> Can you recall how uplifted we were by the presence of God before this young man spoke? But now we feel condemned, don't we? Young man, if you want to bring a word of that kind, bring it to the leaders first, then we will weigh it together to see if it is indeed what God wants to say.

The pastor's words settled the congregation and my friend could preach.

When I heard this story, I was pleased to hear of a pastor who had the courage to correct what he felt was an inappropriate word at an inopportune moment. I was also pleased that by doing this he was able to retrieve the situation and allow the people to continue to enjoy the presence of God and to hear what my friend had to say. This leader took his responsibility seriously, and for that reason I must commend him. But this story left me with some niggling questions.

- Did anyone sit down with the young man to discover his gift and help him develop it?
- Did anyone correct him by helping him to learn the right way to bring prophecy to the Body of Christ?
- Was he left to nurse the wounds of that stinging, public rebuke on his own, disheartened, embarrassed and doubting his gift?

In my time I have fasted and prayed and got what I considered to be a word from God. I have sat there asking, 'Is this right?' I have faced the thought of standing up and delivering something that might not be received. I have delivered words that have been publicly corrected from the platform and felt the burning shame as I sat down afterwards. Thankfully, in my life I have also been blessed with caring people who will not hold back from confronting me, but who equally understand the personal cost: friends in leadership who have wanted to see my gift develop and have encouraged me as well as corrected me.

Called to account

Before we go any further, I should make it clear that Scripture does encourage us to judge prophecy.

> If anyone does not listen to my words that the prophet speaks in my name, I myself will call him to account. But a prophet who presumes to speak in my name anything I have not commanded him to say, or a prophet who speaks in the name of other gods, must be put to death. You may say to yourselves, 'How can we know when a message has not been spoken by the LORD?' If what a prophet proclaims in the name of the LORD does not take place or come true, that is a message the LORD has not spoken. That prophet has spoken presumptuously. Do not be afraid of him. (Deut. 18: 19–22)

There are some key elements here. First, it's clear that God expects us to take prophetic words very seriously, and we will be called to account for what we hear. A word of direction or correction in particular should be weighed, if only for reasons of self-protection. If we find it to be of God, we should be eager to act.

The Scripture is equally clear that just because a recognised prophet says something is from God, that doesn't mean it necessarily is from God. It could be something prophesied out of personal motive, such as bitterness or unforgiveness – such things need discerning and dealing with sensitively. It's even possible that the source could be demonic. Again, careful discernment and sensitive handling are a must.

By the way, just so everyone's clear, while I'm advocating taking prophetic words seriously and weighing and testing them in line with Scripture – and even dishing out some tough love when things are clearly amiss – putting our prophets to death is not an option!

How do we do this practically?

One of the simplest ways to help those pastorally responsible for the church is for the prophets to take responsibility for adjustment and correction of their own kind.

In the New Testament, in the context of the gathered church, we read the following:

> Two or three prophets should speak, and the others should weigh carefully what is said. And if a revelation comes to someone who is sitting down, the first speaker should stop. For you can all prophesy in turn so that everyone may be instructed and encouraged. The spirits of prophets are subject to the control of prophets. For God is not a God of disorder but of peace. (1 Cor. 14:29–33)

There is so much wisdom and practicality in this verse.

1. While individual prophets can control their own activity as prophets, it is equally true that the community of prophets have responsibility to correct each other.
2. Make space for each other so words can be heard clearly.
3. Don't let too much be said without it being weighed. It's far easier to audit a little, and it's less likely to cause you untold damage if there are two or three

words which are considered rather than a cacophony of unchecked words.

4. It allows others the opportunity to discern whether their unspoken words are in line with what has gone before.

This self-assessing should produce confidence and peace among the leadership of a church and its congregation. It's also a key to developing mature prophets rather than mavericks.

I remember being responsible for mentoring a young prophet. Though keen to prophesy, he would regularly make basic errors with his message, his motives, or his presentation. Something he recognised, as did the other prophets in our church. So we agreed that we would work together for a year to develop his gift and deal with these basic errors.

For the first three months, this young man would go ahead and give his word, but always allow me to debrief him and suggest ways he might have done things differently. Then for the following nine months, he would share every word with me, the tone of his delivery and even his personal attitude before he delivered his prophecy.

Often he would have a genuine revelation but the way he expressed it would be condemning, hard hitting or discouraging. So, if he had a revelation, I would say to him, how are you going to bring this, what are the words running through your mind so far?' For instance, he might say something like this:

'The church is not responding to God as He would like. The church needs to wake up!'

I'd then simply point out to him that if he communicated like that it wouldn't be very encouraging – quite the opposite. I'd then offer an alternative. How about setting the word against the wonder of God?

> 'Our God is mighty! Our God is faithful! Our God is power-ful! I want to wake up and sing His praise.'

By doing this, you place yourself as the recipient of the prophecy along with everyone else, not yourself over and above the people. This means you carry the people with you rather than pointing fingers.

By working on the young man's delivery and his discernment as to when it was appropriate to give a word, he became more at peace with himself and more sensitive with his gifting. Not only that, but the pastoral team trusted him more and looked to him for the word of God, rather than getting that sinking feeling every time he got up to speak.

That's a very specific kind of application: it was one-on-one and usually the weighing took place before the person uttered the word or revelation publicly. A more common approach would take place in real time, during a service or prayer meeting. In this situation the other prophets should be trying

1. to sense the common threads and themes
2. to discern what God is saying through the various contributions

In most cases the words given in a gathering are just fine. They may not hit the bull's-eye, but neither does our teaching or our music every week. What we are looking for here is not some kind of perfection but a practical answer to the question: 'Was it by and large okay and reasonably close to the target?'

Equally, we don't need to weigh each word in minute detail. In by far the majority of cases the words will be fine, and weighing is a way of affirming, bringing peace, and clarifying any threads that might be emerging for your congregation.

All this is just fine, provided no one comes out with something really troubling. But what do you do if someone has brought something that is right off course?

I remember being in a congregation some time back when someone brought a deeply troubling prophetic word, which was clearly demonic in its impact and seemed to have its roots in spiritualism.

The leader was obviously taken aback by the force contained in the word. But he composed himself and said something along these lines:

> 'What we have just heard was not from God. I will make it my business to sit down and share with our brother later, but let's now get our hearts focused back on the Lord.'

By taking this course of action he very quickly led the people back to a focus on Jesus, and the damage was limited.

What's equally important is that everyone knew that good leadership had been exercised. We went back to worshipping God and peace returned to the meeting. The weighing of the prophecy had done its job.

While this may seem daunting, with a few simple tests you will be able to handle most situations:

1. *The yardstick of Scripture*
The first test in weighing prophecy is to apply Scripture as our yardstick.

If anything contradicts Scripture, it is clear that it is not of God, and the simple response is to say, 'Actually, what the Scripture says is ...' – and move the meeting on.

If you think it might contradict Scripture but you are unsure, you might want to take a moment with one or two from your leadership team and ask them.

If you are still unsure, simply say, 'We are not sure how that lines up with Scripture. The leadership team will take this away, pray over it and ponder it, then come back with a response.'

If you take this course of action, please make sure you do come back with a prayed-over response. People have very good memories!

2. *The EEC test*

The second test is what I call the EEC test: does the prophecy **E**dify, **E**ncourage, **C**omfort?

If it does one or more of these things, the word is probably safe and on target.

3. *Does it leave me in peace?*

Scripture talks about letting the peace of Christ rule. If something really unsettles you about a word or prophecy, check with others how they feel about it. If you are still uneasy, give yourself space to pray about it and seek God. You'll be surprised how often you'll get clarity about what is wrong and be able to adjust the prophecy or comment accordingly.

Leaders' response to prophetic words

The most important thing I can say here is to appeal for an authentic response to a prophetic word, whatever the circumstances. In other words, a response that is not 'fudged' because of fear or uncertainty. If as leaders we can honour the person and honour the gift, that's a great starting point.

What do you do if the word you hear sounds mixed?

One of the hardest situations to deal with is when a word is given that seems mixed. Some parts you feel comfortable with, while others sit uneasily with you. What you need to do here is to extract the precious from the worthless. Hold on to the parts where it seems God is clearly speaking, while carefully and prayerfully considering the rest. That way, you should leave the giver and the congregation at peace.

What happens when you are unsure about a word?

It is quite legitimate to say to your congregation that you're unsure about a word that has been given. Just make sure they are clear that you are still prepared to take it seriously and pray over it. It is no shame to be unsure. We should all be unsure from time to time. What's important is that you fulfil your responsibility to weigh the word and act appropriately. And make sure you feed back to the person giving the prophetic word, communicating your decision and the process by which you came to your conclusion. If it's necessary or appropriate, you may also share your conclusions with the church.

Also, when you are unsure about a word that is being given, don't be afraid to look around the congregation. If you see heads bowed or shaking or get a general sense of unease or embarrassment, there's a good chance the word being given needs some correction.

What do you do if there is a clear strategic direction brought to the church publicly?

If it is in line with, and confirming, previous prophetic words over the church, it's probably fine. If the prophecy is strongly directive and you have not had a word of that nature before, your responsibility is to take it away and pray it through before responding.

Some years ago, our group of churches was given a prophetic word about going to Europe. At that time we were already sending teams and supporting workers in Uganda, Kenya, Zimbabwe, Nigeria, India, China and many other places. But not in the heart of Europe, so this was a significant prophetic word. As was their responsibility, the leadership team carefully and prayerfully weighed this word. After some time, they were of the opinion that this was a genuine call from God, so they set up further times of prayer to determine the application and practical outworking. A strategy was then put in place for the implementation. Now, several years later, the church has strong links with Europe, particularly France and Poland. We've seen churches planted and significant numbers coming to faith through these. All because in this case that original prophetic word was taken seriously and weighed, and a process was begun to seek God concerning its application.

I had the privilege of visiting Rich Marshall, the author of *God@Work*, and observing him training working men and women to hear God in their places of work. There were around one hundred of us in the room that night, and after giving us some practical guidelines, Rich set each of us the task of hearing God. Within an hour everyone had got something. That was good, but not in my experience extraordinary; what followed, however, was masterful and extraordinary.

Rich had a stack of whiteboards at the front of the room and he asked if there was anyone present who was gifted in art. Someone duly volunteered. He then got each individual to share their revelation, one at a time, while the artist drew up one image that might represent that person's word. As the process developed, what was striking was the number of similar words that could be loosely grouped together. By the end of the 'weighing' process there were scores of images and summary sentences on the board. Somehow or other Rich was able to summarise the plethora of individual words and collate the essence of God's communication into a string of sentences. It was what we call in training circles a 'story board' and it was deeply effective.

To round things off, I want to summarise both the responsibility of the prophet and the responsibility of leaders.

The responsibility of the prophet

1. Be open and make it easy for others to correct you
2. Know for a certainty that at times you will be wrong – even when you passionately feel you are right

In Appendix 2 of this book you'll find what I call a 'weighing matrix'. The idea is to use this for maybe three months or so. Every time you bring a word or feel God speaking to you prophetically, ask at least one leader and two other prophetic people you trust to score you. On that matrix, when someone has given you feedback, ask yourself how you received the parts of the word that were judged unclear or scored low, and see what you can learn from that. It's subjective, and it's not meant to be some kind of foolproof mathematical tool, but it helps to make the process of affirmation and adjustment less threatening for the prophet and 'scorer' alike.

For years I had a pool table in my office and was trying to improve my skills. The only real way to improve with pool is to take shots and see where your accuracy was good and where it was bad. You observe how the cue ball hits the object ball, and you soon see in which direction certain shots will take the ball. You can then correct yourself. If you waited until you could play a perfect shot every time you would never strike the ball. You have to constantly play the shots so that you can learn how to strike correctly. There is no shame in shooting and missing a bit. Very soon, however, you learn only to shoot when you are 90 per cent certain: if you're not too sure you are more inclined to play a safety shot.

The responsibility of leaders

If you are a church leader, you will know that today in the Body of Christ there are wounded individuals who have received so-called prophetic words which have damaged them. There are churches that have been destroyed because of wrongly given, wrongly timed or wrongly implemented prophetic words. I understand the fear in some churches and leaders with regard to the prophetic gift. It can be so destructive. But that fear cannot stay in neutral. I want to encourage you to despise that fear.

From time to time we hear of counterfeit banknotes being found in circulation. Does that mean we don't spend any money for fear of getting fakes in our change? No: we check each note to ensure it's the real thing. The existence of the counterfeit simply means there is actually something genuine and good to be had.

The answer to bad prophecy is not to ban prophesying altogether – to throw out the clean baby with the murky bathwater. What we need to do is take responsibility, to weigh the prophecies that come our way.

> From everyone who has been given much, much will be demanded. (Lk. 12:48)

If you feel you are alone in this or that you need help, then join the rest of us! Feel free to ask for external help if you believe as a leader that you need equipping or training. Just don't let fear overrule your willingness to receive heaven's words through this gift.

On the other hand, there are prophets who have been crushed by the harsh rebukes of leaders who have not understood how to handle what they have heard or how to handle those giving the word.

I want to encourage you to put the ideas of this book into practice, so that prophets, pastors and leaders will not be a burden, a frustration or a pressure to one another, but will become genuine assets to each other in developing gifts and ministries and in serving the Body of Christ.

Leaders, please make sure your prophetic men and women get feedback, correction, affirmation and encouragement. Maybe use the weighing matrix for a short while as a prompt, and do share your own weakness or vulnerability when you don't know. It will help.

By and large, if prophetic people know you appreciate them they will be able to take almost anything from you. Prophetic people need to know when they are spot-on, and they need to know when it was badly wrong. They need to know when you are uncertain and when you are 'parking' a word. They also need to know that you are not writing them off but sharing with them in order to develop their gift.

> Do not put out the Spirit's fire; do not treat prophecies with contempt. Test everything. Hold on to the good. (1 Thess. 5:19–21)

Summary

- Weighing prophecy should be a positive experience for all concerned
- Prophecy should be judged responsibly

- Prophets should be self-policing
- Appropriate response to prophecy should develop the prophet and build confidence in the church
- Prophets and leaders should work together in weighing prophecy

6

Revelation, Interpretation, Application, Implementation

In this chapter I want to talk through what I believe is the most common sequence of events relating to a prophecy. While there are no passages of Scripture that clearly lay out this sequence, I do believe that it is often implied and illustrated.

Given that revelation, interpretation, application and implementation are fairly technical terms, our starting point will be to answer the question: What do we mean by these terms?

1. Revelation

I was working on a marketing clinic with a company's managing director, who was from the Middle East. We were trying to help him describe the process, and then the value and benefit, of what his company was providing. I said to him, 'You have something wonderful and attractive here, but it's cloaked in confusion. Somehow or other we must unveil its beauty.'

He leaned back in his chair pensively. For a moment I thought I had made a cultural blunder of some sort. Then he smiled broadly and said, 'When I married my wife, it was arranged; I hadn't seen her before the wedding. One of the most memorable days of my life was when her veil was pulled back to reveal her beauty and to reveal my future.'

The Greek word for revelation means 'uncovering' – a bit like when a veil is pulled back and we catch a glimpse. We can perhaps see a shape or a form; we might even be able to discern certain features. However, there comes a moment when the veil is drawn back and we see the beauty of the truth.

We could broadly describe revelation as some super-naturally inspired knowledge or information that comes to us through a dream, a vision, an audible voice, a picture, a scripture, a sense of knowing, a seeing or even through a life circumstance.

2. Interpretation

Quite simply, interpretation means making sense of the revelation. It unfolds the meaning. In 1 Corinthians 14, where we read about interpretation of tongues, the Greek word for 'interpret', *hermeneuo,* has the sense of 'explain the meaning of'. In other words, the interpretation will give us understanding of what that person's spirit is saying to God.

3. Application

Application is the unpacking of what I or we have to do with the revelation: what the outcome should be, or will be, in the light of the prophecy. Sometimes this will be personal; at other times it will be for one or two individuals, or a church, or even a group or denomination. Unless the prophecy itself contains an obvious application (which is rare), I will be asking questions such as:

- What response is required of me? (In particular, do I leave it with God and pray it through or is this something I must do now?)
- What practical steps do I need to take?
- What strategic or administrative changes or structures are necessary?
- How do I communicate this and to whom? (e.g. the whole church, a smaller group, just the leaders?)
- How do we lead in the light of this?
- What practical consequences should I be aware of and planning for?
- What is God's timing in all this?

4. Implementation

This final part of the process is about seeing the prophecy fulfilled. It's the carrying out of what God desires. It's the end point of prophecy – something that isn't always reached.

What's important is that all four stages require seeking God.

> Above all, you must understand that no prophecy of Scripture came about by the prophet's own interpretation. For prophecy never had its origin in the will of man, but men spoke from God as they were carried along by the Holy Spirit. (2 Pet. 1:20–21)

A classic example of all four stages can be seen in the following story:

> When Gideon heard the dream and its interpretation, he worshipped God. He returned to the camp of Israel and called out, 'Get up! The LORD has given the Midianite camp

into your hands.' Dividing the three hundred men into
three companies, he placed trumpets and empty jars in the
hands of all of them, with torches inside. 'Watch me,' he
told them. 'Follow my lead. When I get to the edge of the
camp, do exactly as I do. When I and all who are with me
blow our trumpets, then from all around the camp blow
yours and shout, "For the LORD and for Gideon."' ... Gideon
sent messengers throughout the hill country of Ephraim,
saying, 'Come down against the Midianites and seize the
waters of the Jordan ahead of them as far as Beth Barah.'
(Judg. 7:15–18, 24)

Gideon was in deep trouble, but he was also in deep
engagement with his God. The Midianite army had
amassed a huge force including Amalekites and other
troops from the east. Scouts couldn't even count their
camels there were so many. God speaks to Gideon and he
goes off with his servant to listen to what the Midianites are
saying. He hears a man describing a dream, and that is the
moment of revelation. His faith rises and he understands
the interpretation: God is going to deliver the Midianite
camp into their hands. The application is immediate and
he needs to wake up his troops. The implementation is a
mixture of immediate and unfolding. He has an immediate
strategy with torches, pots and trumpets, and a further
implementation which involves getting some more
Israelites to help finish off the job.

Some general pointers

Some prophetic words are straightforward declarations
or exhortations, and no direction or interpretation needs
to flow from them. Others, however, are directional or
strategic and can even be a little obscure. In other words,
we know that God has spoken, but we are frankly unclear

in our understanding of what it all means. As leaders and elders we have a responsibility to apply our giftings, to press through for the interpretation and then for the application and implementation, in whatever time-frame that may be.

Process and outcome are two words that need to be at the top of our vocabulary when we start to look at interpretation and application.

Revelation often carries with it a kind of software programme that is written in heaven's programming department and has an embedded process. The process is part of the journey that starts with the revelation itself. One of the biggest dangers in our culture is the instant-demand mindset, which wants instant words, with instant understanding, instant application and instant implementation.

Revelation, understanding, process and outcome may be separated by some time. Take Moses as a biblical example. Moses has a revelation about being the deliverer of God's people. It takes a journey into the desert to get the interpretation, and a further forty years in that desert before the real application surfaces. If that's not enough, it then takes another forty years for the implementation!

The four stages may be separated by years or even decades. In all of this there is a fundamental principle we have come across before:

> It is the glory of God to conceal a matter; to search out a matter is the glory of kings. (Prov. 25:2)

Naturally, this prompts the question: Why does God do it this way? Here are some answers:

1. The wait and the seeking are often an integral part of the process that the prophecy or dream initiated. It is common for the journey involved to have

as much value as the revelation and subsequent interpretation, application and implementation, if not more.

2. God knows our hearts. He also knows how important it is that we seek him, and he knows how difficult most of us find that. He knows that by hiding the answer, he will cause us to seek him for it, and that as we do so, maybe, just maybe, we will touch his heart and enter his presence in a way we would not otherwise have done.

3. The wait is like that of athletes preparing for the starting pistol, making sure everything is just right before they are catapulted into their real purpose – running the race. Scripture talks of 'the fullness of time' and 'the appointed time'.

Write down the revelation and make it plain on tablets so that a herald may run with it. For the revelation awaits an appointed time; it speaks of the end and will not prove false. Though it linger, wait for it; it will certainly come and will not delay. (Hab. 2:2–3)

It's interesting that this scripture is dealing with the fall of Babylon, some sixty-six years after Habakkuk's prophecy. What a strikingly different timescale to Gideon's experience – though probably closer to the norm.

A reasonable question is, why does God speak the word so early? Why not leave it until six months before, rather than sixty-six years before?

Well, there are several reasons. One is simply that the giving of the word, and the potential seeking of God in response by the recipients, can change the outcome, or at the very least can change our place in that outcome.

A classic case in point is the story of Jonah, who is told by God to prophesy again and again, 'Forty more days and Nineveh will be overturned.' The king then gets the city to give up their evil ways and their violence and to call 'urgently' on God. God sees what they have done, and how they have turned from their evil ways. He has compassion on them, and does not destroy them as he had threatened to do.

Luckily for the people of Nineveh, the time between the word and its implementation was decided by God, not by Jonah!

Another reason has to do with yeast. I love it when my wife, Gill, bakes bread. She starts by mixing yeast and sugar together to activate the yeast. When it froths up, she mixes it into the flour and lets it rise before she knocks it back and lets it rise again. The she knocks it back again and shapes it before she puts it into the oven to bake.

In a way, prophecy is like mixing the yeast of God's word with the sugar of the prophetic gift. This starts off a process that can and should end with the 'bread' of implementation.

Let's look at some scriptures with different processes and outcomes.

> One night the Lord spoke to Paul in a vision: 'Do not be afraid; keep on speaking, do not be silent. For I am with you, and no one is going to attack and harm you, because I have many people in this city.' So Paul stayed for a year and a half, teaching them the word of God. (Acts 18:9–11)

Here we see all four stages in remarkable clarity. Paul is in Corinth, and because of previous experiences elsewhere he is in some doubt about whether it is safe to stay. The revelation itself carries the interpretation, or at least needs no interpretation. It is not very difficult to understand exactly what it means, and Paul gets on and does it. The application was to stay on and to keep doing the job.

One question might still arise: How long and doing what exactly? The implementation over time was that he stayed a year and a half teaching before the next nudge to move on.

Acts 20 gives us a slightly different story, as Paul speaks to the elders at Ephesus:

> 'And now, compelled by the Spirit, I am going to Jerusalem, not knowing what will happen to me there. I only know that in every city the Holy Spirit warns me that prison and hardships are facing me. However, I consider my life worth nothing to me, if only I may finish the race and complete the task the Lord Jesus has given me – the task of testifying to the gospel of God's grace. Now I know that none of you among whom I have gone about preaching the kingdom will ever see me again.' (Acts 20:22–25)

Here is a revelation – it's crystal clear to Paul from the Spirit that danger and hardship await. But take a look at the process, the application and implementation, and then see the outcome, part-right and part-wrong.

Firstly, Paul assumes that the application of this word will lead to him not seeing any of his hearers again. Most scholars agree that it is fairly certain that he did in fact revisit Ephesus.

Next in this journey, Paul and the team land at Tyre and stay with the disciples for seven days. In Acts 21:4 it says, '*Through the Spirit* they urged Paul not to go on to Jerusalem.' Now they too understood, either first-hand or through Paul's own words, that the Spirit was warning about hardship as he went to Jerusalem. They have their own view of the application: *Don't go to Jerusalem!* So they have heard God quite clearly in terms of revelation, and probably of interpreting what it means, but out of their love or need for Paul they give an unhelpful application.

Agabus then comes onto the scene and brings clarity to the application and the implementation.

> Coming over to us, he took Paul's belt, tied his own hands and feet with it and said, 'The Holy Spirit says, "In this way the Jews of Jerusalem will bind the owner of this belt and will hand him over to the Gentiles."' (Acts 21:11)

Again, on hearing this and out of love for Paul, the people plead with him not to go. Finally, in verse 17, Paul actually arrives in Jerusalem, and the implementation reaches another stage:

> The following night the Lord stood near Paul and said, 'Take courage! As you have testified about me in Jerusalem, so you must also testify in Rome.' (Acts 23:11)

We see a fascinating repeat of this process in Acts 27. Paul, acting by intuition or sensing some warning of danger from God, declares:

> 'Men, I can see that our voyage is going to be disastrous and bring great loss to ship and cargo, and to our own lives also.' (Acts 27:10)

Here we have a revelation, but the interpretation and proposed application are not quite right. They did indeed suffer a great storm, but the ship was not lost, and neither were they.

Human emotion, caution or prudence clouded Paul's understanding and the declaration he had given. He added an incorrect interpretation to the revelation.

Now if the apostle Paul can be distracted by events, should we not assume that this will be true for us also, and learn from that?

Later, when the ship is near destruction and the morale of the sailors is low in the extreme after days of storm, Paul says:

> 'Last night an angel of the God whose I am and whom I serve stood beside me and said … "God has graciously given you the lives of all who sail with you."' (Acts 27:23–24)

As for the implementation, when Paul sees some of the sailors attempting to escape he calls to the centurion, 'Unless these men stay with the ship, you cannot be saved' (Acts 27:31). Acting swiftly to cut the ropes that hold the lifeboat, the soldiers are able to thwart the sailors' plan to leave the ship and so save their lives.

This is not a situation that I anticipate I, or you for that matter, will be in. But that doesn't mean there aren't lessons to be learned from these scriptures.

1. The process and outcome took time. The application and the implementation of the word developed from the first revelation and its interpretation, all the way through to Jerusalem, where it was eventually revealed that Paul would end up in Rome.
2. Well-meaning, godly people (even when open to the Spirit) can interpret or give revelation from the heart and not from heaven. Kind hearts and compassion can obscure, cloud and confuse the real interpretation.

In our churches in Basingstoke, two of our most gifted leaders died very young – both from cancer. We fought on their behalf; we prayed and fasted for their recovery. There were lots of words of encouragement and people understandably interpreted those words to mean that these young leaders would be healed.

The problem is simply that the longing of people's hearts, their compassion, led them wrongly to the certainty that there would be healing where sadly there wasn't.

In both cases, added to the pain of loss was the confusion as to why these prophetic words didn't appear to have any substance.

Again, Scripture is not without example. No one should have to go through the suffering Job endured. And seeing this suffering, it shouldn't surprise us that his friends rallied round with words they believed would be helpful. But out of their desire to help and, it would seem, a rigid and wrong theological perspective about God and the place of suffering, they gave the wrong interpretation and application. Indeed, it would even appear that Eliphaz in particular had a rather dubious, or at least confused, mystical experience on which he based his advice (see Job 4:12–21).

Keys to be aware of

1. Understand the process, which begins with revelation.

- Consider weighing the revelation at an early stage: how sure are we that this revelation itself is of God?

- Is there a clear time-frame? Is there a call to wait? Is it obvious when it should be implemented? How do we know?

- Interpretation comes from God. Significant issues may require fasting and will often involve waiting.

- What do we believe God wants our response to be?

- Is the interpretation we've received, or the proposed application, prompted by compassion or pain rather than by the will of God?

2. Weigh any interpretation or application – don't just accept the first one.

3. Interpretation can often be given in stages, so don't assume that the first interpretation you have is the whole thing. Remember, we receive a word, then we look for the interpretation. Then, over time, there is a process and a final outcome.

Incidentally, in my own experience and from what I know of the experience of other people with a prophetic ministry, the aspect of our application and implementation that we typically get wrong is timing.

4. When it comes to the application and implementation, especially of significant corporate or strategic words, the prophets should look to each other for weighing, and ultimately partner with those who have apostolic (or a leadership) gifting.

I remember delivering a report from myself and two other prophets to the leaders of Basingstoke Community Church. Though we all felt the word 'regional' was significant, the degree to which we felt this varied between the three of us.

The document was read and weighed by local elders and by those with trusted apostolic ministries. Very early on, they deemed it to be of God, but the application and implementation were unclear. It was prayed over and taken back to God many times over a six-year period before it was finally implemented.

Personally, I got rather frustrated by the delay – that's my nature. But actually, looking back now, I am so grateful for the careful, considered approach which not only weighed the revelation and interpretation, but which also took careful steps to be sure of God's timing and process before the implementation.

It is interesting to note the role of apostles in application and implementation.

Typically prophets are not good at that, and we may well muddy the water when we try. That's true for me, anyway. I have worked with Dave Richards in the Salt and Light family of churches for nearly three decades. We have travelled tens of thousands of miles together, and I love it when we work together. His apostolic gifting makes room for my prophetic gift and allows me to seek God for churches, for leadership teams and for individuals. While I'm able, thanks to God, to see strategies and direction, the thought of implementing such things makes me anxious and actually hinders my prophetic gift. Dave, however, shines in such situations. He loves to build long-term, to take the revelation and interpretation and sometimes over years see the vision take shape.

I also work with Jonathan Booth, Director of Care for the Family. He too has apostolic gifting. He too loves to build. In fact I remember him saying to me: David, I can't help building; it's what I love to do. He has generously opened the resources of Care for the Family to provide a platform for the prophetic we are carrying together, and over the course of three years Care for the Family is setting up something like sixty regional evening events where the message 'Love Work, Live Life' can be shared. I don't have to be involved in the day-to-day management, which is a huge relief to me. Equally, Jonathan and the team will 'build' around the process.

Summary

- Prophecy contains a process of revelation, interpretation, application and implementation
- The stages of the process may be separated by years, even decades
- Waiting is an important part of the process
- Our natural desire to care and comfort may cloud our understanding
- Prophets need to partner with apostles and leaders – especially to see implementation

7

Dreams

My wife and I had made our decision. We had spent a wonderful nine months working with churches in the USA and had a visa and an invitation to return more permanently. We were very keen to do so, and sensed the leading of God in general to do exactly that. We had placed our home on the market and were waiting to sell it. In due course we got an offer of £75,000 less than the asking price – I flatly refused even to consider it. Then I had one of those moments.

I felt God was challenging me over my attitude to money, and I sensed him saying, 'What's more important, to get the full price for the house or to do my will?' Gill and I decided that we would try to get a bit more money if we could, but in practice we would accept that low price.

We looked on the internet and found a house in the USA. Friends in the States viewed it for us and we decided to put in an offer.

And then I had a dream that would change the course of our lives.

I dreamt I was in a left-hand-drive car in a lot of turbulence on a rough and rocky road. I was driving erratically. Gill and our youngest daughter Cheryl-Ann were in the car. Then I saw an angel standing in the middle of the road, facing us, his skin luminous grey-white and his hand raised towards the car, making a 'stop' signal. The hand became huge and came right up to my face. In the dream a voice said, 'Stop. You don't know what lies round the corner.' Then I saw some heavy construction equipment digging foundations of what I assumed was a motorway that did not yet exist.

When I awoke, I was profoundly moved and deeply frustrated. Moved to have seen and heard what I took to be an angel. Frustrated, because all he seemed to be saying was stop, without any reason or any sense of whether this was to be permanent or just a delay, or indeed anything practical that I could do in the meantime.

I shared the dream with Gill and one or two trusted friends and we all agreed the interpretation had to be that we call off our intended move to the States. This was confirmed rather amusingly by the potential buyer of our house coming back and offering us even less!

The problem for us was that it gave us no other direction. It hinted at something big, not ready yet, round the corner, and it seemed to involve Gill and Cheryl-Ann, who was still at home. It also left us with financial difficulties, which were due to be resolved with the house sale. And finally, it left our American friends very disappointed.

Since that day, through an amazing set of circumstances, God has seen to it that a new 'motorway' has been built, enabling us to deliver the 'Love Work, Live Life' message on the workplace. I have had two meetings with the Minister of State for Youth and Community Development in Singapore looking at Work Life Effectiveness, worked with Focus on the Family and the Billy Graham Evangelistic Association, and seen the release of the new book *Love Work, Live Life*. After the very first UK 'Love Work, Live Life' event sponsored by Care for the Family, I emailed Rob Parsons and Jonathan Booth to tell them it felt as though we had cut the tape and the new motorway was opened.

If Gill and I had moved to the States, little if any of this would have opened up. Even more important has been the journey for Cheryl-Ann. In an amazing way, linked to our physical location near Basingstoke, she has found her own walk with God and is rooted into the local young people's group.

And in all of this we have been able to keep up and develop our links with churches in the USA. That dream was in July 2003, three years ago to the day as I write these words.

What I want to share in this chapter is something close to the heart and mind of God and one of his primary ways of speaking to men and women, young people and even children: DREAMS.

We all have dreams

If your immediate response is, 'I don't dream', or 'God doesn't give me dreams', I would ask you to open your heart as you read this material.

Back in the early nineties, I had never thought about my dreams. I had them, but took almost no notice of them and by and large forgot them as soon as I woke up. Then I had the privilege of listening to John Paul Jackson, who shared in a very practical, down-to-earth way about dreams, and something that day changed my attitude completely. It was as if a switch was flicked on and my dreams suddenly became a source of God speaking to me.

Since that day, my life, my destiny and my faith have been significantly impacted by dreams.

As we shall see, God promises uniquely to speak to his children directly through dreams. And there is an unexpected richness and breadth of Scripture devoted to dreams.

Though we may not always be aware of it, apparently we all dream – without exception. And if you look over history, the world has been significantly shaped by people responding to their dreams.

Einstein was inspired to discover the theory of relativity through a dream. Niels Bohr came up with quantum theory after a dream. Bernard Matthias invented the superconductor in his sleep. It is the realm where Newton, Edison and Goodyear received insights for their discoveries and inventions, which have affected the lives of millions.

Alexander the Great was about to conquer Jerusalem when two dreams stopped him suddenly. In one he saw the high priest in his robes. That same night the high priest of that great city had been told in a dream of his own to put on his robes and meet the conqueror. When the priest arrived in his robes, Alexander met him just as in his dream and fell prostrate before him, to the consternation of his fellow officers.

In 1940, when the Second World War was already raging in Europe, a young engineer called David Parkinson at the Bell Telephone Company in New York had a dream about anti-aircraft guns. In his dream, the most successful gun had a device attached to it that looked just like a piece of equipment he had developed for charting telephone data. On waking, he realised his device could be adapted for use on such guns, so he set about working on it. The device he developed improved the accuracy of anti-aircraft guns and in the last months of the war was used with life-saving effect against German flying bombs over London.

Does God really speak through dreams?

'For God does speak – now one way, now another … In a dream, in a vision of the night, when deep sleep falls on men as they slumber in their beds …' (Job 33:14–15)

Dreams can come to us in many forms. They can be 'visions of the night', or as in Job chapters 4 and 7 they can become disquieting dreams and nightmares. Dreams are also ephemeral: they fly away easily (Job 20:8). In other words, if we don't make an effort to capture our dreams, they are soon lost to us. That's probably the real reason why so many people say they don't dream.

And let's also remember that while these scriptures and others show clearly that God will speak to us through our dreams, they also make it clear that the natural biology of the human body can produce its own dreams, as can the stresses and concerns of life. Having said that, of course, we should note that God can use any dream we have to speak to us.

Be expectant

I pointed out earlier in the book the significance of Joel's prophecy about dreams and visions, and the promise that came through Peter's use of Joel's words on the day of Pentecost. This is the age of the Holy Spirit, an age dripping full of prophetic activity. But equally, it should be a time full of dreams.

Just as the original Greek language of Acts 2 implies that the prophetic gift should be in frequent use, so we should be experiencing more and more in the realm of dreams. That should be our expectation and our experience.

It's our time to dream.

Why does God use dreams?

This is an important question to ask. After all, dreams can be some of the strangest experiences we have.

Here are some of my thoughts on the matter:

1. Dreams are a promise for all people in these last days. They are promised in the Old Testament and again in the New Testament, with a clear indication that this promise is for our time also.

2. They are a primary way for God to speak without our active interference and without effort on our part. After all, we are asleep! This is grace in action – while we sleep, God speaks to us, without our effort or prayers – we don't even have to fast!

3. By their very nature, dreams urge us to seek God for the answer and not depend on our own. Most of us find it hard to press in and seek God, but a dream seems to give us an impetus to seek God. There is intrinsic value in the process of searching. The seeking process can be as important to our spiritual development as the dream itself.

4. Dreams bypass our reason and our ability to argue. Dreams can actually give us revelation that is totally different to our opinions. However open we think we are, it can be difficult for God to speak against our own strong opinions in any other way.

5. Some dreams – particularly significant ones – speak directly to our spirit. They are etched into our spirits.

6. Dreams get beyond our minds. They get beyond our current knowledge and experience and open our minds to future possibilities. I have seen some wonderful things in dreams, things I never would have conceived because they were outside my frame of reference.

In dreams, God is speaking his word or responding to our requests for wisdom, clarity, direction or understanding.

A dream is a series of images impressed on the subconscious mind. It is an appearance, an apparition, or a mode of revelation which is something like the reflection in a looking-glass.

A dream can be something reflected, as it were, from God into our mind. It will not be a perfect word, but it will impact us like a form of heavenly reflection. Our own mind then processes that information in very different ways.

Let me demonstrate. When I say the words, 'green grass', what do you see?

You may think that all people everywhere will see the same thing. But the fact is, 'green grass' will conjure up all kinds of images that will be different for each of us. Some will see a white picket fence with neatly mown grass. Some will see fields of tall, flowing grass stretching into the distance. Still others will see hills with green grass at the summit and white flowers blooming.

God uses the difference to get across to us what he wants to reveal.

Different kinds of dreams

> God gave knowledge and understanding of all kinds of literature and learning. And Daniel could understand visions and dreams of all kinds. (Dan. 1:17)

There are dreams of all kinds. What might some of them be? We are going to look briefly at some of the main ones and see what we can learn from them. Incidentally, these are illustrative and not definitive. These are not a series of specific categories; they are glimpses of opportunities and possibilities. There are around thirty types of dream in Scripture, probably more, which John Paul Jackson covers in his CD teaching resource *Basics of Dreams, Visions, and Strange Events*.

1. A warning

> God came to Abimelech in a dream one night and said to
> him, 'You are as good as dead because of the woman you
> have taken; she is a married woman.' (Gen. 20:3)

Warnings are generally immediate and pretty clear. I
remember one night having a vivid dream in which
a fox was brutally savaging a panda. I could see the
terrible damage the fox was inflicting and I could even
see into the muscles and the bloody, open abdomen of
this poor panda. It was shocking and got my full
attention.

But what would that be about?

To you and me it may seem strange. But remember,
God uses images that speak to us personally. My son's
favourite cuddly toy was a large and endearing panda. It
went to bed with him every night. When I woke, I knew
the dream was about the children. The fox immediately
prompted a scripture:

> The little foxes … ruin the vineyard. (Song 2:15)

I knew something was trying to ruin the family. What was
the fox doing? He was biting and devouring the panda.

> If you keep on biting and devouring each other, watch out
> or you will be destroyed by each other. (Gal. 5:15)

This was a warning to me as a father. At that time, the
family was abnormally engaged in picking on each other
verbally and unkindly, and I knew I was responsible
for not dealing with it. Sharing the dream and the
scriptures helped to bring order and peace back into the
relationships.

2. Protection

> 'I know you did this with a clear conscience, and so I have
> kept you from sinning against me. That is why I did not let
> you touch her.' (Gen. 20:6)

Let me tell you about Ricky, a college student from our church in London. In a dream, Ricky saw a young person screaming, as if they were being tortured. The dream was horrific at first; the cries were awful. Then God handed Ricky a key. In the dream she opened a door, and then light flooded the room of the tortured girl. Jesus stood there and an amazing peace filled the room.

Ricky called us to ask what to do. We suggested she took some time to pray. A while later she came back to us, convinced that the dream was for one of her classmates.

Though it was a tough call, Ricky decided to talk to her classmate. The conversation that ensued wasn't easy, but it ended with the friend tearfully admitting that she had had an abortion that no on knew about. She hadn't been able to tell a soul, not even her own mother.

As a result of that dream-led conversation, she came to the post-abortion counselling centre in Basingstoke and got some help. But the story did not end there. A year or so later, on Christmas Eve, we got a phone call from Australia. It was Ricky's friend telling us that she had given her life to Christ. What a wonderful outcome.

3. Destiny

> He had a dream in which he saw a stairway resting on the
> earth, with its top reaching to heaven, and the angels of
> God were ascending and descending on it. (Gen. 28:12)

I remember some years back visiting a young man from our church together with my friend Dave Richards. He had been admitted to hospital with suspected meningitis. While he was in hospital, he had a dream of a white marble bridge. He knew God was challenging him to choose his destiny. At the time he was far away from God, and although we gently challenged him to respond he said he wasn't ready to pay the price. Not long afterwards, one of this young man's great heroes died, which began a process that led him back to God. Now twenty-five, he is leading a small church, running a business and discipling a number of families. Nine years ago I don't think he would have believed that possible. But a dream was a significant marker in the outworking of God's hand of destiny on his life.

I love the story in John Pollock's book *George Whitefield and the Great Awakening* about the time when Whitefield is wondering about his future. He is in awe of his bishop (Dr Benson) and has a dream in which he is talking with him in his palace. The bishop gives George some solid gold. The book recounts that George 'soon forgot the dream about the Bishop's gold'. The following January, however, he was summoned to see the bishop, who told him that even though he was below the age at which the bishop had determined men should be ordained, he was willing to ordain George whenever he felt ready. Then the bishop picked up a purse and handed Whitefield five guineas in gold, with which to buy a book. George suddenly recalled the dream and his heart was filled with a sense of God's love.

4. *Business strategy or insight*

I remember running seminars around the UK for the Marketing Guild. At the end of the seminar, delegates were asked to sign up for a free thirty-day trial. At venue after venue, delegates were not signing. I knew the service inside out and there was no conflict in my mind about its value or the appropriateness of asking people to sign up for the free trial. I asked a few intercessors to pray.

That night I had a dream in which I saw two pages of paper with typed sentences. I woke up quickly, wrote down what I had seen, and asked the conference manager Barbara to type them up and put them on an overhead. I used the overheads in my presentation and something like 60 per cent of the companies signed up that morning! When they had all left I sank to my knees and praised God for his faithfulness. God had given me a strategy in a dream as some intercessors had faithfully prayed.

5. *Direction*

Ulf Eckman, the pastor of Word of Life Church in Uppsala, Sweden, had a dream of a train going from Sweden to Russia. He thought it probably had a simple and spiritual application: his church should regularly send teams over to Russia. One year later, the Soviet Minister of Religious Affairs gave a train to Word of Life for one month. In May 1992 the train went through eleven towns in Siberia and 5,000 people were recorded as giving their lives to God. In June 1992, because of the response in the town of Abakan, a Canadian evangelist called Peter Junger went back and another 50,000 were saved.

6. *Soul expression*

A dream comes when there are many cares. (Ecc. 5:3)

Sometimes dreams are a reflection of what's going on in our soul. If I am getting anxious it is quite common for me to have a dream about a seminar going wrong. I know it is an underlying anxiety that I haven't yet taken to God and dealt with.

I read somewhere that John D. Rockefeller was the first billionaire. He made a million a week in oil. He gave away money in dimes. By the time he was 33 he was a millionaire, but at the age of 55 he became very ill with a serious disease. He lost all his hair and began to look like an old man. His stomach was so weak that all he could eat was crackers and milk. Everyone knew he was going to die soon. In fact, a monument to him had already been prepared and a grave was ready to receive his body. Then he had a dream.

He dreamt that when he died, he could not take any of his money with him. So he decided that he had better give it away while he was still alive. He started to give away thousands and then millions. And as he gave away his money his health improved. He lived to 60, then 70, then 80, and finally died at 97! The dream had revealed to him the state of his own soul, and it produced significant change.

7. Solution and invention dreams

Gill and I stayed at a beautiful ranch near Sturgis, Michigan, set in hundreds of acres of wonderful grounds. The ranch was built by a poor family for use by people in God's service who needed rest and recuperation. Probably like you, I was intrigued to find out who owned it and how they could afford it. This is what I discovered.

In a series of dreams a man from a poor family with limited education got a series of numbers, which he wrote down. He had no idea what they were, so he asked a friend, who told him it seemed like a chemical formula. His friend helped him get it patented and subsequently found that in the dreams God had given him a formula for a certain type of acrylic which was used, and is still used, by NASA in their space programme. I visited the factory in Sturgis (RAM) which until 2005 was still producing the acrylic.

8. Dreams for evangelism

In the north of England there is a church-run shop called The New Rainbow. At the back of the shop is a little table with a sign: 'Psalm Reading.' Lots of people misread it as 'palm reading' and ask what it's all about. Then I guess they get asked for a number between 1 and 150 and a psalm is read. Also at the back of the shop is another sign: 'Dreams Interpreted.' Some twenty people have given their lives to Jesus as a result of having their dreams interpreted.

I was sharing this story in one of our churches. I remember coming back to my seat, sitting next to a lady who was obviously agitated. I asked her if she had had a dream that was troubling her. She told me that she wasn't a Christian but wanted to come to this Sunday gathering to seek God. The previous night she had had a dream in which she was led to believe that if she went to church her daughter would be taken ill. I asked her what she thought the dream meant.

'Someone or something doesn't want me to come to church,' she said, 'and they want to frighten me off.'

I asked, 'Do you think that's likely to be God?'

'No,' came the reply.

Very gently we prayed together, asking God to bind any attempt by the evil one to frighten or influence her. Some months later I had the joy of hearing that this lady had given her life to Christ.

So there are many kinds of dreams. Dreams that will reveal the state of relationships; dreams that will show life vision, or national, even international, events. There are dreams to encourage, and dreams to prepare us for national disasters and give us strategic solutions. There are dreams in which God gives us answers, and dreams in which he shows us how he will provide.

In the next chapter I want to continue looking at dreams, asking the question, how do we interpret our dreams?

Summary

- We all dream
- God uses our dreams to speak to us – if we will let him
- Be expectant – it's our time to dream
- There are different kinds of dream:
  - *warnings*
  - *protection*
  - *guidance*
  - *insight*
  - *direction*
  - *soul-revealing*
  - *problem-solving*
  - *evangelistic*

8

Interpreting Dreams

I have travelled with John Paul Jackson and seen scores of people in place after place wanting him to interpret their dreams. I can understand that: I have the same desire for interpretations myself. Whenever I preach on dreams, there is always a queue of people afterwards with questions, but more commonly people desperately wanting interpretations.

The last time I preached on dreams was in a large church in Oxford. It was an amazing day. One man travelled from Birmingham because the night before, he had had a dream in which God told him someone was talking about dreams in Oxford and he needed to be there! The service finished around 12.30 p.m., but there was still a line of people waiting to talk after 2 p.m.

Though I'd love to help all these people, as would John Paul, the truth is neither he nor anyone else can interpret all dreams. In fact, the real truth is that God is the source of dreams and he is the source of their interpretation. Knowing this lessens the burden. You and I can be grateful that God is the source and we don't need to walk around being able to interpret any and everybody's dreams.

'Do not interpretations belong to God?' (Gen. 40:8)

Interpretation of dreams is not immediately or automatically ours. Even those practised in interpretation cannot interpret every dream, as Daniel made clear. As you probably recall, Nebuchadnezzar has a dream which he wants interpreted. He refuses to tell the wise men around him what the dream was, but still promises the death penalty for failure to interpret it. Keen to preserve his life and those of his three friends, Daniel seeks God for many hours before the mystery is revealed. As Daniel knows,

> 'There is a God in heaven who reveals mysteries.'
> (Dan. 2:28)

So our starting point is this: We have to seek God, ask God, and hear from God.

Writing your way to clarity

By my bed I have what Gill calls my dream machine. It is a little gadget which has a notepad and a space pen in a small holder. When I get a dream I pull the pen out and a small light comes on to illuminate the notepad. I can then write the dream down. The space pen helps because in theory it can write at any angle. Gill bought it for me so that I would stop waking her up by turning on lights and rummaging around for pens and paper in the dead of the night.

When I get a dream, I don't want to wake up fully. I have to urge myself to get a grip on whatever it is I have been dreaming. The truth is, if I don't write something down, most of my dreams are forgotten by the morning. So the way it works with me is this: I wake up groggy in the middle of the night or at the end of my sleep and I have the faintest recall of a dream. I can usually remember the main scenes or the basic gist of the dream. If I can't remember that much, I can usually recall one or two moments. At that point I force myself to write down what I can remember.

At some later stage I begin to quarry the information. Quarrying implies time and effort to keep digging until you find the coal or gold you know is there, but you can't quite see as yet. What I mean in practice is that I dig deeper and ask God to help me unearth the detail that I have forgotten. I am asking for more, looking for more and writing down what I get.

Writing down dreams was a biblical discipline. Daniel wrote down the substance of his dreams. The Spirit, speaking to the apostle John, says:

> 'Write, therefore, what you have seen, what is now and what will take place later.' (Rev. 1:19)

At the time, a dream can seem so vivid that it's easy to think you don't need to write it down. But sure enough, in the morning, if you are like me at least, you will find you can't remember a thing.

It is so easy to forget. A dream is like a furtive nocturnal bird, appearing and suddenly disappearing again before we can get hold of it. It must be caught before it escapes, before the day's activity stirs the mind. So write it down!

I remember receiving a very short dream many years ago, in which a Swedish entrepreneur came to me and offered some money to start a business. I wrote it down in my prayer journal – just one sentence. Then I simply forgot it. Around two years later, my wife and I were struggling in our business. A primary income source had dried up and we were struggling for survival. In the middle of this process, as we were seeking God for a solution, a Swedish entrepreneur came and asked if I would start a company for him if he put in all the money. I was not at all sure if this was right, and while praying it through I flicked through my prayer journal and came across the dream. What confirmation!

Writing in itself will sometimes clarify the interpretation. In other words, as I write the dream and quarry the details, the interpretation becomes clear to me.

David said this:

> 'All this I have in writing from the hand of the LORD upon me, and he gave me understanding in all the details of the plan.' (1 Chr. 28:19)

As we write, sometimes the hand of the Lord will come upon us and give us understanding at that moment. But of course that's not always the way, and for very good reason.

I had a dream

For months I had been preaching out of Ezekiel chapter 47, along the lines that when the river hits the sea a number of things are happening, and yet more will happen. The river was seen as a metaphor for the move of God we had been experiencing. The sea, in my mind, represented the unchurched or unsaved and the church reaching out into the world:

- Swarms of living creatures – life everywhere: 'Everything will live'
- Large numbers of fish – because the river flows there
- Fishermen along the shore
- Places for spreading nets
- Fish of many kinds
- Nourishment and healing in abundance

At some point during these days I had a dream. In the dream I was travelling towards the sea; I could smell that wonderful salty smell and sense that sticky sensation on my skin, just as you would when travelling to an English beach. But we were not quite there. Between where I stood and where I knew the sea to be were rivers flowing fast, incredibly clear and beautiful, full of luxuriant underwater growth. There were underwater plants the like of which I have not seen in real life.

There were wonderful fish, clearly visible, swimming in this magnificent water. And above the river were swarms of insects – 'life everywhere'.

As I looked, I saw that along the banks all the way to the sea there were houses. Each house had a veranda or decking immediately next to and overlooking the river. On the verandas were teams of men looking intently. The dream zoomed in on one house, and on the veranda was a team of men with two senior leaders from our network of churches, Barney Coombs and Steve Thomas. The group was gathered round a large machine – somewhere in the region of six feet high and three feet wide. On each decking around these machines there were identifiable leaders from different streams or denominations.

As I wrote this down I sought to see further what the machine was, and my understanding was that it was a machine capable of stitching leather. The river was driving the machine and no human hand was involved. I sensed that it was leather wineskins being divinely produced by the river – right at the point where the river was about to enter the sea.

What was the interpretation and how did I arrive at it?

The first question I asked was, who was the dream for? Who was at the centre of the dream? The answer to that question was our own church leaders and one or two from other spheres. In our case the two individuals were quite significant. Barney Coombs is the senior leader of the international team, and at that point no one had been formally appointed to lead the European team – Steve now has that responsibility and I think the dream was confirming that move.

In a more general sense the dream pointed to a time pretty well upon us. The houses all along the river were representative of the various spheres or charismatic church streams in the UK. The timing was now or very soon – i.e. as the river gets to the sea. The inference I drew from this was that somewhere, out of this current move of the river of God, new wineskins will emerge from each stream or movement, fashioned by the process of the river itself. It is as if we shall see the hand of God do it. The time for looking out for that emerging wineskin is as the river begins to reach the sea, in other words as the recent moves of the Spirit in our churches find their expression in touching the unchurched.

What use is a dream like that?

Well, it is giving a clue to senior leaders that out of the recent moves of the Spirit in our land we should be aware that God wants wineskins (church structures and forms) that are initiated by the Holy Spirit. Different wineskins that as leaders we facilitate and observe and respond to, rather than feeling we have to control or manufacture them.

I shared this with Barney and Steve, and with one or two other prophets to get their perspective on it and to have it weighed.

Variety in interpretation

The interesting thing about dreams is that there is so much variety in the way in which God gives us interpretation.

Sometimes the interpretation is obvious or is given with the dream itself. The dream about the Swedish entrepreneur is a case in point. I knew the individual, and the dream was unambiguous. In other circumstances it could have been a parable or a metaphor, but in this case it was straightforward and clear.

Sometimes the sense of what the dream means begins to unfold as we write it out. Writing is almost a form of meditation: as we think, pray and reflect, the meaning can emerge. The river dream we just looked at would be illustrative of that process. I know that quarrying out the detail will often reveal the key or keys to unpacking the meaning. In the case of the river dream, the fact that the water was driving the machine and that it was producing leather wineskins without leadership intervention was a key to unlocking the meaning. Those details only emerged as I wrote down the dream and asked God to reveal them.

Sometimes God hides the meaning. I simply do not understand quite a number of the dreams in my journal. We've already mentioned the 'hide and seek' nature of God, and yes, he does love to hide things, partly to encourage us to seek him for the answer. It may well be that some dreams are intended to be parked, so that as we mature we may then get an interpretation. With some dreams, the timing involved in the uncertainty is in itself a part of the process.

On rare occasions, a supernatural encounter may unlock the meaning and the process of dreaming. In my experience, seeking for the interpretation somehow facilitates that encounter. The most obvious case would be Daniel setting himself to fast and pray. He seeks God for an interpretation and after twenty-one days he gets an encounter with an angel who unlocks the meaning of his dreams and visions.

Practical pointers to interpretation

When we are looking for an interpretation there are some practical pointers to follow, and I am indebted to John Paul Jackson for teaching us these (for more information see John Paul's teaching resources on dreams at www.streamsministries.com).

1. Interpretation comes from God

There are plenty of Freudian methods to interpret dreams. Some contain so-called dream alphabets. But God deals with each of us in unique ways, so there is no chance that one system would work for each of us. There's real safety and wisdom in that.

The starting point is to turn our mind Godward. Having asked him to help bring clarity, the next thing I ask is this: 'Who is it for or who is it about?'

If you are the centre of focus in the dream, then the dream is about you and for you. If you are not the focus but you are participating in it, then the dream is likely to be primarily for others, though it may involve you.

One secondary question here would be, 'What's my role?' Am I to pray this through or does the dream require some form of response from me?

When you are not in the dream at all, it is likely to be something not directly related to you, e.g. a church, a town or a nation.

Another question to ask is, 'What kind of dream is this?' Is it a warning? Is it an insight? Is it direction?

2. Remember that dreams are usually symbolic

It is best to view dreams rather in the same way as parables. Don't get into too much detail, otherwise things can get very obscure. Look for the overall view. *What is God trying to get me to comprehend?*

So, for example, the issue is not in the detail of the mustard seed or what type of tree it becomes. The essence is that something very small becomes something very big.

If we look at a familiar story from Genesis chapter 41, where Pharaoh has a dream about seven pairs of cows, half fat, half gaunt, and then a second dream about seven ears of corn that are healthy followed by seven that are scorched by the east wind, we get a good example of how to go about interpreting a dream.

Joseph is asked for an interpretation. He addresses the question, who is the dream for or about? He articulates what the main theme is. And having done all that, he then comes with clarity to suggest to Pharaoh a strategy for dealing with the national warning God has given. We are treated to a mini-seminar on interpretation here: Joseph teaches us that the same dream is given twice in two different forms (in this case at least) because God has determined to do it and it's about to happen.

A team of us were travelling in the USA doing prophetic and dream workshops. In one of the workshops a lady shared this dream: she was standing on a mountain, declaring the word of God and surrounded by God's people, and then three figures approached her and tore at her clothes.

The team leader, in an appropriate setting, asked her a couple of questions, in particular what was her emotion or feeling as she woke up. Not unexpectedly, she said she felt anxious and insecure.

The interpretation was pretty straightforward. She had a ministry of the Word with God's people, but regularly fear, depression and anxiety (the three figures in the dream) would metaphorically tear her clothes and cause her to lose confidence, and become ineffective in her ministry. The team prayed that she would be set free from such concerns.

Having sought God first ourselves, and only then, it is legitimate to ask one or two others to seek God with us if we get stuck. Sometimes someone unrelated and without the clutter of knowledge can get to the heart of the dream faster than we can ourselves, because of our detailed knowledge.

3. What kind of symbols?

Here we begin a journey into the vague, the esoteric and the strange. One of the most common questions asked at workshops is *what do various symbols mean?*

To start with, Scripture can give us a clue as to what symbols and pictures mean. The fox in my dream prompted me immediately to think of the Scripture, 'The little foxes ... ruin the vineyard.' In Scripture, bread, seed and manna all symbolically refer to the Word of God.

Often commonplace things in our experience form the basis of the dream language for us. So when God tells Gideon to go with his servant, the dream he hears someone describing is about a barley loaf. Gideon was a miller of barley, so the interpretation of that dream for Gideon with his occupation would have been fairly straightforward.

Symbols will mean different things to different people. If I see a dog in a dream it is usually threatening or dangerous. To one of my friends, a dream about a dog would have a homely, safe connotation. This is where keeping a journal becomes important, because as you record dreams with particular images and their interpretation it is quite likely that you will build a history of what symbols mean for you.

What follows is a partial list, which John Paul Jackson first helped me with and which has become, to a degree at least, part of my world.

Transport

- Bikes and motorbikes can often refer to ministry or sphere of gifting. It is usually in the singular and usually mine
- Cars can likewise refer to ministry or sphere of operating, but this time involving a small group or team
- Buses could mean reasonably large churches. Planes or huge ships might relate to church streams or denominations

Buildings

- A small house might represent your own sphere
- Bigger buildings might represent churches or groups
- Large office blocks might represent church movements or streams

Creatures

Scripture is full of imagery concerning animals, so if you dream about a horse you might care to look at references in Scripture to horses.

- Horses speak of power, often national power
- Snakes, unsurprisingly, are likely to represent the demonic, or lies, or seduction
- A spider might indicate a web of intrigue or a hidden trap; it can also indicate an occult presence
- Hornets, bees and wasps are likely to be harbingers of pain and damage

Weather

- Dark foreboding weather is likely to be the enemy or the enemy's plans
- Bright weather with blue skies is likely to be the favour of God or hope

Please note: these symbols are illustrative, not definitive. They are examples, not a checklist. The most valuable thing about them may be that they will open your mind to see how symbols of your own could work for you in a very simple and natural way.

The key is keeping your dreams in a journal. Ideally, they should be word-processed so that you can easily look at them and in years to come even cut and paste them into records of different types of dream. If you're diligent in keeping those records, the fruit will be an increased understanding of what various images or symbols mean to you. It is wonderfully rewarding to go back over the many times God has spoken to you through dreams.

Having said all this, we need to avoid the extreme of basing our whole life on dreams. The book of Ecclesiastes reminds us:

Much dreaming and many words are meaningless.
(Ecc. 5:7)

Dreams are wonderful, but the contrast between them and the written Word of God is like Jeremiah's contrast between straw and grain.

Scripture also reminds us not to take an unyielding stand on dreams. Colossians reminds us of the danger of getting puffed up with supernatural encounters, which lead to us ultimately losing connection with Christ the head and then with the rest of the body. That's why being accountable and working with other prophets and leaders is important. Any significant or directional dream needs to be weighed. That is a simple precaution against lurking deception.

Some common questions

1. Are all dreams from God?

The answer is an unequivocal no. Too much pizza or wine can produce dreams. Remember Scrooge in Dickens' *A Christmas Carol* – too much cheese! Chemicals, medication, stress or anxiety can all produce dreams. These are the body's wonderful way of handling those things. Watching films or plays can often produce violent or sexually-orientated dreams which are the body's way of processing that material. Unforgiveness or buried anger can also produce dreams that are quite often violent, and commonly troubled.

It is also possible for the enemy to throw the odd dream in our direction. Dreams from the enemy leave you feeling agitated and ill at ease, but prayer will soon put that right.

Sometimes you get tiny dream fragments: just small, almost meaningless, frames or images. They don't seem to be body-induced but they are there. I mused on this and came to the conclusion that they are 'tuning'. I play the guitar a bit, and when you tune the string you go a bit high, then a bit low, then bang, it's in tune and your mind knows it's there. I think these fragments are little tuning moments: a bit high, then a bit low, then bang, a dream emerges.

2. How do I know which dreams are from God?

How you feel when you wake will give an indication as to the source of the dream and its intention. Usually great fear or disturbance is a sign that this dream is from the enemy.

Others we will be unsure of, and so we write them in our journal and reflect on them occasionally, and see if anything from heaven emerges over time. It's fine if nothing does. That is the nature of seeds: some die, some live.

With some dreams we will be strongly aware that they are from God and so we log them in our journal and seek interpretation and application. Hebrews reminds us that the mature 'by constant use have trained themselves to distinguish good from evil' (Heb. 5:14). In other words as we process, weigh up and reconsider, it becomes progressively easier to determine whether a dream is from God or not.

3. How often is it normal to dream God-given dreams?

We are told that everyone dreams nightly but few remember their dreams. Very few people I know dream godly dreams nightly. I certainly don't, and I don't think I could cope if I did! There are seasons when you will dream every night; some people dream a few times a week, others dream a few times a month and still others a few times in a year.

Frequency is not a measure of godliness – but it is quite legitimate to ask God to speak through our dreams as we settle down for the night.

4. What does it mean if I dream the same dream twice or more?

We looked at Pharaoh's story and Joseph's comment that 'the reason the dream was given to Pharaoh in two forms is that the matter has been firmly decided by God' (Gen. 41:32). The same dream twice, or in this case two different dreams about the same outcome, is an indication of definiteness. God is doubling the intent to get our attention. Some people get similar dreams night after night. What it may be is a sequence, rather like the acts of a play, with parts of the whole story unfolding as it goes on. Or it could be looking at the same thing from different views, rather like Ezekiel's four faces giving four different views of God – the lion, the ox, the man and the eagle. Sometimes dreams from different angles will give us a more complete perspective.

Numbers reminds us of God's word to Aaron and Miriam:

> 'When a prophet of the LORD is among you, I reveal myself to him in visions. I speak to him in dreams.' (Num. 12:6)

Since the first dream in Scripture, dreams, visions and interpretations have been among the primary sources of God's wonderful prophetic word. Let's treasure them. Let's allow God's Holy Spirit to tune us in to our dreams. Let's be encouraged to seek prophetic dreams.

It's our time to dream.

Summary

- We all want our dreams interpreted
- Interpretation comes from God
- Keep a journal of your dreams to help you to remember them and interpret them
- God uses symbols we can relate to – so look for the obvious
- Not all dreams are from God

9

Variety is the Spice ...

If there is one thing I'd point to that characterises much of the prophetic in the charismatic and evangelical world today, it would be 'sameness'.

Most of our experience of the prophetic is through personal words, and words given in a church gathering. And while I don't want to despise any prophecy, the truth is, that's not the way it's supposed to be.

The Bible is rich in its prophetic variety. It's literary, dramatic, artistic, sensory and symbolic. Prophecy is a creative endeavour. And we need to rediscover this for the twenty-first century.

It's as if we've stayed black and white in a colour age. We're analogue while everyone else is digital; one-dimensional in a multi-dimensional universe.

It is my firm conviction that prophetic people need to get ahead in communication, in art, in drama, in work and in family. We have a powerful potential to affect a culture for God, and it needs variety if we are to achieve this.

I know there are prophetic personalities in straight-jackets reading this – *please be released to be who you are.*

One God, one Spirit, one Word, many voices

Scripture is consistent on one thing: the remarkable variety of prophetic gift and its diverse applications and manifestations.

> There are different kinds of gifts, but the same Spirit. There
> are different kinds of service, but the same Lord. There are
> different kinds of working, but the same God works all of
> them in all men. (1 Cor. 12:4–6)

As we take a tour of this diversity, be open to having your
our own uniqueness and creativity stirred and released.

Abel is the first prophet recorded in Scripture and he
prophesied through his workplace. His offerings were a
prophetic forthtelling that all productivity of the flock is
from the Lord and belongs to him. The Lord loved this
and looked with favour on Abel.

Joseph dreamed, and through God could interpret the
dreams of others. He had a strategic and administrative
application to his gift. He was promoted to head of
Potiphar's house, then governor of the prison, before finally
becoming Prime Minister, because of the way his prophetic
gift made room for him in his working world.

Miriam, the first recorded prophetess, took a tambourine
and led the women in dancing and spontaneous singing.

Moses laid his hands on the elders for the Holy Spirit.
He performed miraculous signs and wonders, and did
awesome deeds with mighty power. He knew the Lord
face to face. He wrote and sang songs.

Deborah led a nation, and brought military strategy to
it through her gifting. She was an amazing motivator.

Samuel was attested as a prophet of the Lord. God
let none of his words fall to the ground. He heard the
audible voice of God and was set aside to serve God in the
temple at an early age. He confronted kings. He engaged
in symbolic and dramatic acts, including pouring out
water before the Lord, fasting, and setting up a stone as
a physical geographical marker of how far the Lord had
helped the Israelites.

A group of prophets, presumably in Samuel's training school, came down from their high place with lyres, tambourines, flutes and harps being played before them.

Elijah confronted the prophets of Baal with all kinds of dramatic and supernatural acts, such as calling on God to set fire to a bull that was saturated in water and laid on an altar. He performed miracles, including raising a dead child and calling down fire from heaven. Elijah was an intercessor.

Elisha (Elijah's disciple) also performed miracles. A widow was saved from destitution when he got her to bring pots and pans that were subsequently filled with oil. He raised a young boy from the dead. He neutralised poison in a communal dinner. He fed a hundred people from twenty loaves. He gave Naaman God's prescription for healing. He could see the hidden forces of heaven.

Nathan was a wise man, a person of insight and a military advisor to the king. He oversaw the planned succession from David to Solomon. He confronted the king when he sinned with Bathsheba. He had an ability to bring a confrontation prophetically through parables.

Gad, along with Samuel and Nathan, kept written records.

Ahijah ripped his cloak into twelve pieces on meeting Jeroboam, symbolising the break-up of his kingdom.

Isaiah walked naked and barefoot for three years as a symbol that Egypt and Ethiopia were to be taken captive at the hands of Assyria. He saw amazing creatures in the heavenly realms. He called on the Lord successfully to make the sun's shadow go back ten steps on the stairway of Ahaz.

288 sons and relatives of Asaph, Heman and Jeduthun were set aside for the ministry of prophesying, accompanied with harps, lyres and cymbals.

Ezra and **Haggai** were inspirational preachers whose words brought motivation to the workers rebuilding the temple.

Jeremiah made a yoke out of straps and crossbars and wore it to depict an impending Babylonian bondage. He bought a linen belt, wore it and then buried it until it had rotted, before finally digging it up to illustrate the word of God to the children of Israel. He watched a potter at his wheel and used the scene as a prophetic metaphor. He subsequently bought a pot and broke it as part of his prophetic word.

Ezekiel made a model of Jerusalem under siege. He lay on his left side for 390 days and on his right side for 40 days. He was commanded to shave his beard and hair and scatter some of it as a dramatic prediction of the scattering of a portion of the Jews to various parts of the earth. He dug through a wall and he remained dumb for seven days, identifying with the pain of those to whom he would minister. He prophesied to dry bones, to the breath and to mountains.

Daniel was a strategist, a wise man and a member of the main political think-tank of his pagan government. He dreamt and could interpret dreams. He had supernatural encounters with angels and angelic princes. He foretold the long-term future right up to the end of history.

Hosea was commanded to marry a harlot and name each of his three children as a prophetic statement. He was ordered to be reconciled to her and he bought her back. He prophesied judgement with great literary richness.

Joel, Amos, Obadiah, Jonah, Micah, Nahum, Habakkuk, Zephaniah, Haggai, Zechariah and Malachi prophesied the future in different ways, using an amazing variety of literary content. They each, however, had different emphases. Joel focused on a day of judgement, while Amos called for social justice and condemned all who make themselves powerful or rich at the expense of others. Obadiah spoke of Edom as a recipient of God's punishment. Jonah got to travel and prophesy in foreign lands. Micah walked around barefoot and naked, making strange animal noises. Nahum was poetic. Habakkuk wrote a dialogue between himself and God. Zephaniah was a socialite and wrote with great political awareness. Haggai and Zechariah encouraged the returned exiles to rebuild the temple. Malachi wrote an oracle.

There is also variety in the prophets' modes of operation:

Elijah and **John the Baptist** were strongly individualistic, voices crying in the wilderness, although even here they had their disciples.

There were **prophets** attached to the royal courts, and others attached to the temple. In today's world that might be the equivalent of some prophets working primarily in the gathered church setting, and others reaching out into the workplace and the community.

In the New Testament, we have the **Magi**, who were prophetic seers from another country, travelling to bring their gifts to acknowledge the birth of the Christ Child.

John the Baptist followed a strange diet, wore very strange clothing and had a prophetic ministry which was to be the forerunner of Jesus, baptising people and bringing them to repentance.

In **Simeon** and **Anna** we see the patience of the prophet, waiting for decades for the Christ they knew would come. They both prophesied over the baby Jesus.

Agabus prophesied symbolically with a belt which he put around Paul.

Barnabas was an encourager who would seek God with others for church planting strategy and human resource deployment.

Judas (Barsabbas) and **Silas** were preachers and encouragers.

John was a mystic and an apostle, who wrote down the amazing revelation he had seen, rich in symbols.

Finally, **Jesus** accepted the title prophet and he embodied virtually everything we have described in the list of prophets we have looked at. He was a prophet *par excellence*. He could see into the heavens, used prayer to great effect, and performed miracles, including raising the dead and feeding five thousand people. He used amazing communication styles, including parables, questions and stories. He loved the common people and he was the exemplar in only saying what he heard the Father say.

The point of this short Bible journey is to demonstrate the variety in personality, in social standing, in message, in embodiment and in the dramatic or literary forms used to enhance or reveal the message.

Now you've seen the variety, ask yourself:

- Does one of these individuals resonate with me?
- Is there a favourite character here?
- Could it be that my spiritual genes are similar to those of one or more of these individuals?

Varieties of impact

Not only did these prophets have variety in the way they prophesied, they also had variety in the way they impacted individuals, communities, nations and the world:

Inspiring: for example, Peter on the Day of Pentecost delivering an inspired prophetic utterance.

Warning: Agabus would be a classic example, warning Paul what would happen on his journey to Jerusalem.

Giving strategy and direction: good examples would include Daniel, Joseph, Haggai and Barnabas.

Writing: Isaiah, John, Shemaiah and Iddo.

Singing and dancing: Miriam.

Consoling: Habakkuk.

Devotional: David.

Weeping: Jeremiah.

Exhorters, encouragers and messengers: Judas, Silas, Ezra and Zechariah.

Judges: Deborah, Amos and Jonah.

Actors or dramatic prophets: Ezekiel, Agabus, Jeremiah and Ahijah.

Moral prophets: Hosea.

Musical or instrumental prophets: the sons of Asaph.

Shepherd prophets: Amos.

Personal prophets: Agabus, Elijah, Ahijah, Elisha and Nathan.

As you scan through this list, I encourage you to think what possibilities you could align with. Notice too that many of these men and women were not limited to one style or mode – variety was part of their lifestyle. It's hardly surprising, given that the Holy Spirit is a creative, inspiring spirit.

Variety in nature and expression

The prophets were steeped in prayer. They were steeped in the Law. They were conversant with the writings of their contemporaries and those who had gone before them. They were also steeped in the creation around them and in the world of everyday things. It is overwhelming to do any form of study on the pictures they used and the images they drew from, because they were so rich and varied.

Take any chapter in Isaiah, for instance, and find glorious prophetic writing drawn from creation and everyday life. As I am writing this I have taken one chapter at random: Isaiah 44. But just look at the list of imagery we have in half of one chapter:

Womb, water, thirsty land, streams, dry ground, pour, spring up, grass, meadow, poplar trees, flowing streams, write, hand, rock, idols, treasure, blind, craftsmen, blacksmith, tool, works, shapes, hammers, forges, hungry, carpenter, measure, line, outline, marker.

The beauty of such language in the prophetic word is that it enriches it. It gives it substance and makes it delightful to listen to or to read. Isaiah could have simply said, 'God is great, he will tolerate no other gods, and all you who make idols are doomed to destruction.' But that language would not have carried the heart of God, the creativity of God or the impact that God wanted the words to have.

It goes without saying that as prophetic people we will do well to be steeped in the Word and in prayer. But we should also be seeking to engage with creation, with everyday life and with work. For some that may mean an engagement with art and literature. For many, it will mean regular time spent outdoors, drinking in nature, whether that be the drama of the countryside or the vastness of the ocean. It will mean exposing ourselves to the different kinds of weather, to times of day and changing seasons. Know what creation is about, for this will tell you about the Creator behind it. Such things will enrich our minds, enrich the content of our prophecy and enrich the experience for our hearers.

Be inspired by Jeremiah, the creator of beautiful phrases, which, though not as powerful in English as they are in Hebrew, are truly magnificent all the same:

> Blessed is the man who trusts in the Lord ... He will be like a tree planted by the water that sends out its roots by the stream. It does not fear when heat comes; its leaves are always green. It has no worries in a year of drought and never fails to bear fruit. (Jer. 17:7–8)

In contrast, Daniel writes his book from his workplace perspective. He starts with historical narrative but ends with apocalyptic language. This is because Daniel, with his gifting, is seeing visions and dreams full of symbolism mixed with supernatural encounters with angelic beings.

What we can take from this, and any extended study of these things, is that variety in our spoken word and in the way we communicate starts with us.

It starts by us seeing the diversity that is God.

It starts by putting ourselves in places and situations where we take note of those things around us.

It starts by letting the Holy Spirit draw from our immersion in creation and everyday things.

It starts by asking God to make our prophetic gift more creative.

There is a danger here, of course, in that we can look for a striking delivery just to be different. That's not the point I'm making. We are looking for a Spirit-led, sensitive but creative development in each of us.

I want to suggest some practical exercises here. Start by praying and asking God to open your eyes, mind and faith to variety and creativity so that you can serve others better with the gift he has given you.

If you are using this book in a group, this is a great moment to stop and pray for one another.

We are going to do a little exercise now to help you develop your prophetic gift. It's a practical exercise that you can do in two parts. In Appendix 2 of this book you will find two simple forms to help you: a creation journal and a workplace or home journal.

1. Within the next three days, spend at least one whole hour in creation somewhere. Go for a walk. Write down everything you see, and as you write it down, visualise it.
2. At work (or home) do the same thing. Over the course of a day, jot down the images that stick in your mind, and as you write them down, visualise them.

Now, in your prayer time, remind yourself of these images. If God gives you a word for a house group, an individual, a congregation or someone at work, ask him to help you draw from your fresh image bank and let it enrich your delivery.

If there is any danger with this exercise, it is that we could add something to the word just for the sake of the exercise. That is a possibility to guard against and to be open with others about. But it is more likely to increase your clarity and sharpness, and to enrich the experience for the recipients.

You can also get a better idea of your own gifting by studying the prophetic style and action of various biblical prophetic figures and seeing how closely your own matches them. See Appendix 2 E, 'Prophetic variety', at the end of this book for a handy checklist to make this easy.

When you've had a go, ask a friend or church leader to look over the list of prophets and let them suggest which one(s) they think you might be close to. This is not a psychometric tool, nor is it in any way conclusive or definitive, but it may just give you a glimpse of types of impact or styles of delivery that you could work at or at least try.

Personal words

As I said at the beginning of this chapter, the one area of prophetic ministry that has received huge attention in the last two decades is the personal word. Often mixed with a word of knowledge, this kind of word is one that excites large numbers to attend big gatherings in the hope that a well-known name will give them a word. While in many ways there is nothing wrong with this, and for some (especially those rare people who do actually receive a word) this can be a positive experience, the truth is that nowhere in Scripture are we urged to seek such words from other people.

One of the problems is that for some, the lack of a personal word leaves them feeling second-class and unwanted. I have also counselled businessmen and women who hold pages of personal, predictive prophecy concerning their businesses, which frankly has only led them into a frightful state – often getting angry with God.

On the other hand, there is a powerful scripture in which Paul gives Timothy the following words:

> Timothy, my son, I give you this instruction in keeping with the prophecies once made about you, so that by following them you may fight the good fight, holding on to faith and a good conscience. Some have rejected these and so have shipwrecked their faith. (1 Tim. 1:18–19)

It is clear from this passage that when we have received a personal word, if we have weighed it and accepted it, we are to follow it in order to fight the good fight that God has called us to. Those who have rejected their words have shipwrecked their faith. I find this scripture amazing. If I were God, I simply would not have put it in Scripture, because the potential for immature saints to follow whacky words has to be high on the list of possible outcomes. But it's in there for our good, and for a purpose.

I was recently with a group of twenty or so mature prophetic men and women. I asked them, 'How many of you have a number of significant prophetic words that have shaped your life, similarly to Timothy's experience?' All but one in that group had several such words, and would have been the poorer without them.

When we receive a personal word, there are some ground rules to follow:

1. Don't immediately embrace it. Write it down and pray over it. Weigh it yourself and weigh it with others, especially a leader whose judgement you trust. Ask, does this bring assurance and peace? Does it align with what God has already been showing me?

2. Ask, what is my responsibility in this? Biblical prophecies will be fulfilled. But these personal prophetic words are often conditional upon our involvement and our obedient, faith-filled action.

3. Am I now able to take action with faith, or am I still unsure? Uncertainty is a response to take note of, because it means you are not fully convinced that this is the clear word of God. Unless and until you are, don't act on it.

4. Most importantly, the person giving the word should talk with the recipient, and ideally with his or her pastor, and get their feedback. Was it accurate? Was it clear? Did it bring peace, or confusion?

If we come to the conclusion that this is from God, we can fall into a couple of traps:

1. We can take no responsibility. This attitude simply relies on the sovereignty of God and damages our responsibility to act.
2. We can end up in a kind of total dependence, allowing personal words to become as important as the written Word of God, or even more important, in our thinking or focus. Personal words that are deemed to be of God do need to be followed, but not in blind ignorance and not without normal common sense operating in our lives.
3. We can think: whatever will be, will be. If it's God's will, this will happen and I cannot change it or any component of it. Frankly, that kind of attitude is a cop-out.

Personal words and evangelism

This is a wonderful arena of opportunity and one I encourage all prophetic people to practise.

My friend Andy was driving by a railway crossing, between business appointments. An old gentleman was standing by the railway line on his own. Andy sensed God saying, 'Go and tell that man about me and lead him to me. Tell him I love him.' Andy didn't respond, and drove off. But the Spirit would not let him go. Andy turned the car round and drove back, then got out of the car and said, 'At the risk of sounding stupid, I want to tell you that Jesus loves you.' Andy shared the gospel with this man and he gave his life to Christ. Then he told Andy the reason why he had been standing by the railway line. His wife had died the year before and he was going to put his head on the railway line to commit suicide. If Andy had not responded to the prophetic prompting to bring that simple but effective personal word, Percy would now most probably be dead.

I earn my living doing a variety of things. One of those things is yacht hire for conferences and parties. I have to admit it's not my favourite job, and I usually get others to run them.

I recall a stag party that had been booked. I certainly didn't want to run it, but there were no other skippers available. I woke early on the Saturday morning with a filthy attitude. As I left the house, Gill encouraged me to change my attitude, or else. Somehow that didn't help. When I arrived at the marina I began preparing the yacht, trying to tell myself that this wasn't so bad – then to my horror I saw the stag party arriving. Fourteen crates of beer, five bottles of wine and more! And these guys were big – seven of them, all rugby players. One of them was bodyguard to Noel and Liam Gallagher of the rock band Oasis. My attitude got worse.

We sailed for the morning and the lads drank a bit, so by the time we got to lunch my plan was in tatters. I had intended to drop the bathing ladder and give everyone a swim, but they had drunk too much for this to be safe. Then the penny dropped. I was sitting on a yacht with no route out, with seven big guys and nothing to do! I cried out, 'Help!'

I then did the next thing that came to my mind, and asked the groom to say one positive thing about each of his six friends. To my utter relief, it was very moving. Then I asked each of the six to relate one memorable thing about Charlie, the groom. That too was moving. Then, to my horror, one of then said, 'You've been with us all morning. You tell us one thing about each of us.' With a silent but very heartfelt cry for help I asked the Lord to give me a prophetic word for each of them. With my heart in my mouth, I gave it my best shot. When I got to number three he started to cry.

Afterwards, he followed me down into the cabin afterwards and said, 'You probably noticed I have been careful with the alcohol. I'm going to church tomorrow for the second time in my life. But when you started to say those things, something in me wanted to cry. I felt a strange presence.'

His name was Matt. After we had said our goodbyes, Matt asked if we could meet for dinner. We did that, and for eight or nine weeks after that we met for breakfast. Matt would read his Bible and come armed with questions. Somewhere in those weeks Matt gave his life to Christ and some months later he was baptised. The trigger? A personal word from a very imperfect Christian.

Summary

- We would do well to encourage more variety in prophecy
- Scripture is full of creative, prophetic giftings
- There is variety in message and prophetic style
- There is variety in the impact of prophecy
- It will help us if we are steeped in Scripture, prayer, creation, life and work
- We need to be who we are

10

Releasing Prophecy
in our Gatherings

A word for leaders

If we are going to see prophets and the prophetic grow, then we will need to make space for people within our church gatherings and empower them, so that they feel at liberty to exercise what are God-given gifts. Only when we are successful at this will we see communities and nations impacted by the prophetic.

In this chapter, I want to unpack practically how we release the prophets among us. The first two areas I want us to consider ('Making room' and 'The big mistake') are primarily aimed at those of us who are leaders of churches. The remainder are for those of us who are potentially bringing prophetic words.

Making room

What we honour, we tend to get more of. What we welcome is likely to keep turning up. You must have experienced this. You go to some homes and your hosts ooze hospitality. They love visitors, and whatever state their home is in, you feel loved and welcomed. Those are the homes you will visit often. Those are the homes you will return to time and time again.

Contrast that with homes where people are too stressed or busy to welcome you. You know that they are nice people, but somehow they simply cannot make you feel welcome. These are homes where there is a lot going on, homes with activity, jobs and projects, but in all of that, unintentionally, they fail to welcome you. By and large, if you have the choice you will not go back there.

I think our gatherings, especially in the western charismatic and evangelical church, have become busy – there's too much emphasis on 'doing' and not enough time 'being', waiting on God, allowing space for the Holy Spirit to lead us.

For most gatherings, in any church culture, we make room for music, notices and teaching – and not surprisingly, most weeks, that's what we get.

Do we have the same expectation, the same preparation and the same room made for the gifts of the Holy Spirit?

In many church streams, the quality of music and singing provided (usually by a rock band) is now world-class. What used to be a new or rare thing is now commonplace in our congregations. While this may seem like a good thing (and in many ways it is), it's actually one reason why in some church streams celebrations are no longer attended in the numbers they once were.

Now before you get a bit nervous about where this is heading, let me say up front that I have no problem with music bands in a gathering, *but* ...

Bands are loud. And that can mean they're not that conducive to creating an atmosphere in which many will feel like contributing prophetically. Who can compete with guitars and drums driven through a PA system? The fact is, while the music is great, in some settings bands may work against my active involvement. They are a performance medium and it needs gifted leadership to move a group from performance to participation – to get them to allow space for others to contribute their gifts.

At a celebration level, because of size and setting, the big band may be utterly appropriate and even culturally desirable. As I said, the band isn't a particular gripe I have, it's simply illustrative of the point that we may need to rethink the way we run or control our gatherings.

If we want the flow of the Holy Spirit, if we want to be edified, encouraged and comforted, we need prophecy. If we want prophecy and the other gifts of the Holy Spirit, we need to welcome them, make them feel at home and have enough 'un-busy' time for them to feel like visiting.

A good question for a leadership team or group to ask is: How can we make room for these wonderful gifts and ensure that there is time and an appropriate environment or atmosphere for prophecy to happen?

You could ask your prophetic people how easy it is for them to bring a word into the setting you currently have. If they are comfortable, you may have nothing to change, but if they are not, then maybe some things need to change.

I think the starting point is achievable and reachable. As a leadership group, or an eldership, you can table a question or two for your next leadership meeting's agenda. The question is: Do we believe we welcome the Holy Spirit and his gifts in our gatherings? Do we actively encourage our church members to seek God and then bring what they have? And do our gatherings, in reality, make that easy?

If you are unsure, or if you don't think you do, then pray about what should change. What you make room for you stand a chance of getting.

I don't have one pattern to offer, because I don't think that's how the Spirit works. But I do passionately want to encourage leaders to think this through and pray it through.

You might want to have the band switch off from time to time and encourage the band members to break out of performance into their own contributions. Having band members regularly contributing vocally can be a wonderful catalyst for the body to offer their contributions.

You might want to have training sessions for the musicians and meeting leaders, where you discuss and agree ways in which you can make the setting conducive for contributions from the floor. Try different ways, experiment in your setting until you find something that does work.

Once a month, you might want to run a different style of gathering where the structure is either totally or partly open-ended and based almost entirely on 1 Corinthians 14:26:

> When you come together, everyone has a hymn, or a word of instruction, a revelation, a tongue or an interpretation. All of these must be done for the strengthening of the church.

Many seasoned Christians do find gatherings boring. One reason is because the vicar, the pastor, or a select and regular few are always the ones contributing. This scripture says that *everyone* has something to contribute, and that this corporate dimension to gathering strengthens the church. If you want God-breathed variety, encourage it and give it room.

You might want to ensure that gifts are regularly practised as a matter of course in your cell groups and home groups. You might want to sit with prophets you trust and encourage them to bring words in your various church settings. Then, as leaders, whenever you get gifts contributed in gatherings, especially prophecy, do weigh them, do receive them, and do publicly affirm them.

Give time for people to respond. In other words, if you are changing the framework of your gatherings, don't expect the prophets to give you a world-class performance on day one. Interact with your prophetic people during the process of adjustment. Work through it together and be willing to adjust and adapt together.

In larger gatherings, celebrations and the like, a different approach again is needed. If your church has been running such meetings, you will almost certainly by now have a number of recognised, gifted prophets. Ask them how they would like prophecy to be handled in gatherings. Get them to seek out, work with and encourage others to share prophetically. If you find yourselves disappointed with the substance or quality of what you are getting, talk with the mature prophets and pray about it together until you find a way through.

Again, determine that you want to welcome both the Holy Spirit and his gifts.

The big mistake

The next issue to face is a theological issue which I believe, and have seen from experience, is a common barrier to prophecy. It has to do with the gift of tongues and the confusion it can bring in a gathering.

Tongues are a wonderful gift. I love it, use it daily, and would not be the person I am without it. While all the other gifts build the church, this is the one gift given to build ourselves up. Having said that, there's no doubt that it can have a profound impact in the corporate setting. When one or two people bring a tongue in a gathering – when it is interpreted well – it releases, stirs up and moves the prophetic people in that gathering. It's like a catalyst.

But it's at this point that confusion creeps into the church – and with that confusion a blanket of restraint seems to settle, rather than the tongue being a catalyst. The confusion is to do with the nature of tongues and interpretation.

Often, when an interpretation is brought, it is given as a prophetic word or a word from God. That is wrong; it is confusing and it will rein back the prophets. Let me make this as clear as I can. Every New Testament reference to tongues and interpretation shows that they are *to* God, not *from* God.

> For anyone who speaks in a tongue *does not speak to men but to God*. (1 Cor. 14:2)

1 Corinthians 14 goes on to convince us that when we speak in a tongue *we are speaking to God, praying to God, giving thanks to God*. Even on the Day of Pentecost the tongue-speaking disciples were 'declaring the wonders of God'.

What about interpretation?

> For this reason anyone who speaks in a tongue should pray that he may interpret what *he says*. (1 Cor. 14:13)

Why is it that so often when a tongue is given publicly the interpretation comes back as a prophecy from God? I think the answer is simple, and in terms of releasing the prophetic, I believe getting this right can be a tipping-point in many congregations. What can happen is one of three very simple things:

First, the tongue releases or stirs up the prophets, and a prophet will bring his or her message because they sense the pull of the Spirit to do so. But if that prophet understands what we are talking about here, all they need to do is wait for the interpretation first. It's not that their prophecy is wrong; it just needs to wait a minute or two.

Secondly, there is often a misunderstanding of the use of the first, second or third person in English. Let me illustrate. A person gives a tongue; it seems to have the Spirit's presence around it. The person about to give the interpretation gets the sense that it is about God as a rock, a fortress, a strong tower, a refuge in which we can hide. So that person may bring it like this. 'The Lord says he is a Rock, he is a strong tower, a refuge. Come to me and hide in me.'

The likelihood is that the essence of the interpretation is right; it has just been brought inappropriately as a prophetic word. The interpretation could have been correctly given in the second person, like this: 'Lord, you are my rock, you are my strong tower, you are my refuge; in you I can hide.'

This may seem pedantic. On the face of it, it appears such a small difference – and I agree. However, the prophets may be waiting, asking themselves, was that a prophecy or was it the interpretation? What happens, then, is that the Spirit is invariably quenched. And often instead of order and release we see confusion and restraint.

The third thing that can happen (and this is less common than the other two) is that it is simply an error – a prophetic word that is off-target, or an interpretation that is off-target.

The leadership must respond in each of these three cases. In the first instance, the nature and Godward direction of tongues and interpretation need to be taught and reinforced with practice.

With the first issue, the leader might want to say, 'I think that was a great prophetic word, but we have not yet had the Godward interpretation. Let's just wait for that – is there anyone here whose heart is pounding or who believes they have that interpretation?'

With the second, the leader may let it go and gently instruct the person afterwards. Or he can say, 'That was a great interpretation, but it's been given like a prophecy.

Just so we are clear, the tongue was not a word from God, it was Tina declaring who God is from her Spirit. She was declaring God as her rock, refuge and strong tower.'

Just bringing order and clarity like that will almost certainly release the prophets to prophesy.

In the third case, the leader might say, 'That was a good prayer, but we don't have the interpretation yet, so let's just wait and see if God will release that to us.' Or he might say, 'What was just brought was not the interpretation to the tongue, so let's just wait and see if God will release that to us.'

Getting this area right will bring confidence and consistency to what otherwise can be like a wobbly tooth, never quite sorted out but bringing distraction until it is.

Motives

We have briefly addressed leaders and their role. But what about the rest of us? If we want good words, words that really do encourage, comfort and strengthen in our congregations, our motives need to be right.

One of the things I increasingly understand is that God is interested in our motives – the genuine reasons behind the things we do.

Proverbs 16:2 tells us, 'All a man's ways seem innocent to him, but motives are weighed by the Lord,' and 1 Corinthians 4:5 says that God will 'expose the motives of men's hearts'.

If we can allow our motives to be discipled, if we can open up and be vulnerable with them, then the release of the gift in the congregation and in the wider world can be exponential.

It could be that one of the reasons why God has given us the book of Jonah is to show us how easy it is to have impure motives, even when God chooses to give us a powerful, clear, accurate and dynamic word. For someone with the capacity to hear God that Jonah had, his motive was shocking – totally centred around his own ego, his own status. He wanted his word more than the salvation of the people. He was actually afraid of the goodness of God, which would make him look small, or so he thought. He was far more concerned for his own reputation and standing than he was for the people.

Because the prophetic gift is primarily vocal, God will often deal with us more harshly. Why? Because of the power of the tongue to cause chaos.

Many of us with prophetic gifting or temperament will fail sometimes (maybe even often) with the words that come from our mouths. We are quite capable of prophesying with power on Sunday and swearing at work on Monday. And this is not just a problem of the weak-willed. What about Peter, one minute bragging about his allegiance to Jesus, then disowning him (with bad language) to save himself? So take heart, we are in good company and God will see to it that as our foul, fearful or lying words expose our motives, in his grace he will deal with those motives and gradually help us to produce a tongue that is at least becoming a little bit like a spring of clear water.

James 3 shows us that none of us has a perfect tongue.

If our tongue is a rudder, we can inspire and direct our life or that of the church.

If our tongue is a fire, we can commit spiritual arson in seconds.

The church badly needs our rudder-like contributions. But if we take James seriously, we'd better expect God to deal with our tongues when they catch fire, or when they expose our hidden motives.

The word 'motive', or 'motivation', means an inner drive or the reason behind a course of action. We all carry degrees of mixed motives, but the earlier in our development some motives can be met and challenged the better.

Have a quick glance at some potential motives and score yourself on a scale of 1 to 10. If you believe you have almost no trace of a particular motive, score 1. If you think this motive describes you accurately, score 10. Ask a spouse, friend or church leader to score you as well – just make sure you are in a good humour when you do it! Then discuss with your mentor, friend or church leader what these scores might reflect and what you could do about them.

Motivation to move in the prophetic:

- to prove my spirituality
- to be noticed and to receive affirmation and praise
- to try to emulate a man or woman of God whom I admire
- to establish my reputation
- to be a big shot as a prophet

What is a pure motive? One motive, as in the Parable of the Talents, would be obedience. But an even higher motive is love, simply bringing the word so that it does other people good.

> Each one should use whatever gift he has received to serve others. (1 Pet. 4:10)

> Follow the way of love and eagerly desire spiritual gifts. (1 Cor. 14:1)

If we can see our mission as loving and serving God's people, the prophetic word will begin to come more freely and more purely. Love people, and God will see to it that the word will come. Shift your emphasis subtly to hear the prophetic word so that you have something to bring, and you may find it comes with less regularity and with less power.

A good question to ask is not, what's in it for me? but rather, what can I bring for them? A friend of mine, Paul Petrie, taught us to pray, 'Lord, give me bread for my friends.'

Timing

How do I know when to bring a word, or whether to bring it at all?

A good starting point is this: *Don't assume that when God speaks to you, that's the time for you to speak.*

Prophesying at any old time in a gathering is not really on. A few questions as self-checks are healthy here:

- Is this word for me or the church?
- Is it something I have not resolved myself yet?
- Is it for now or later?
- What is the Spirit's mood or manifestation and does my word fit in?
- What theme or direction is the meeting taking at present?

These are questions to ask and keep on asking, questions to practise, so that in time and through experience, through getting it right and wrong, you will learn when to speak.

One common issue that will not help is having some unresolved area in your own life which you then project onto others. For instance, let's say the Spirit has convicted you about forgiving someone. It's no good prophesying something like, 'The Lord is calling you to a greater level of forgiveness.' People will see through this and you will have done yourself a disservice.

The effect

What's the desired outcome of a prophetic word when we bring it?

Paul tells us that it should have a fourfold outcome: strengthening, encouragement, comfort and edification (building up).

One of the ways to check on yourself with the accuracy of litmus paper is to ask yourself whether your word will bring this outcome. Sometimes it's not the word itself, but the way we bring it.

I have been in some prayer meetings where a prophetic person might say, 'I feel we've been praying totally in the wrong direction all evening.' That is so discouraging, even if it is right. You might say instead, 'I wonder if we could pray really effectively into this now.'

If you are using your weighing matrix, these questions will appear, but ask yourself: does my word condemn, accuse, demand or discourage? If you feel the word has done one or more of those things, take it back to God and ask how you could have done it differently. Share it with another prophetic person or church leader for their input and adjustment.

Presentation

We need to remember that we will receive truth through our own set of filters, and we can interpret God speaking to us in a certain way because of our prophetic tendencies.

For instance, we may well receive a word that is sharp and cutting in its effect on us. If we offload it in the same manner to the Body of Christ, we will bruise tender people, wound the meek and unnecessarily offend others. There are times when a sharp word or even one that causes offence is appropriate, but it is very definitely the exception and not the norm. The thing to remember in our churches is that our people are basically 'God's people'. With encouragement, they actually want to receive God's word; they don't need whacking with it! So if we can learn to digest truth and then regurgitate it in a manner which is attractive and edible, we shall do them a favour.

If I am preaching, I will on average spend at least twenty hours preparing each hour of new material. That time includes seeking God, studying, reading, writing and then rewriting. A good chunk of that time – maybe a third – will be spent on packaging that word. By that I mean thinking about the hearers, thinking through examples, stories, visual aids. Why do I do that? Because I want to do the best I can for my hearers. I want them to find it easy to follow, easy to believe, easy to receive, easy to remember. Remember the previous chapter on variety. Don't be trapped into walking out to the front, picking up a mike and just speaking the word. That may be fine, but do keep alert to the possibility of variety. How could you string different images, metaphors, ideas together? Is this a word that would benefit from visual aids – drama, songs, testimony, PowerPoint, paintings, music?

Let me encourage you to trust people to correct and instruct you as well as to affirm. Make it easy for leaders to question, ask, correct and instruct. If our motive is pure we will keep on having a go, knowing that we will get it wrong from time to time. We'll be prepared to pay the price of nerves or embarrassment, knowing that our mistakes or failures will be the foundation for future success.

Summary

- We need to build welcoming spaces for prophecy
- We need to keep an eye on our motives
- We need to learn timing
- Prophecy should be strengthening, encouraging, comforting and edifying
- Don't just focus on the words; think about how you will present your prophecy

11

Taking the Prophetic
to Work

I was walking around the observation platform of the
Menara Tower in Kuala Lumpur, doing the tourist thing.
In my hand I held an audio tour guide: you stand at a
numbered point on the platform and when you press a
number it plays the commentary for that station. I got to
station 12 and experienced something I will never forget.
I was looking out over the city full of mosques and the
commentary went like this:

> In the fourteenth century Indian traders came to our land
> and showed us by their faith and lifestyle that we could be
> freed from the shackles of Buddhism. So we embraced their
> faith, their language and their culture, and have done so to
> this day.

Seven centuries of conversion to Islam because of working
men and women living out their faith prophetically in a
working setting.

In fact if you ask any informed person about the reason
for Islam's strong presence in certain African nations,
they will point you to the traders and shopkeepers who
shamelessly and consistently live out their faith through
their work.

The Sprit at work

We live in a truly incredible era. There has never been another like it in the history of our little planet. Today the move of God's Spirit is indeed global. You cannot travel anywhere where there is a church without coming across people talking of or experiencing the Holy Spirit.

You cannot have a move of the Holy Spirit without the release of prophecy. It's a gift that always accompanies the move of the Spirit. It is estimated that there are 400 million Spirit-filled believers worldwide today. That is a potential of 400 million people prophesying! If 5 to 10 per cent of those believers have the gift of prophecy, we are looking at 20 to 40 million prophets in training, waiting to be unleashed on a needy church and an even more needy planet.

It is offensive and a nonsense to suggest that the Holy Spirit, with his infinite wisdom, power, creativity and marvellous mind, is limited or will limit us to operating primarily in a church gathering, a church meeting or a church context.

For centuries, the church has been like a sleeping beauty. She exists, she breathes, and, for the few in the world who see her potential, she is beautiful. But she has been impotent, ineffective and to a large degree lifeless. Slumbering in a world of need.

A teaching called Gnosticism was the poison that put her to sleep in the first place. This essentially taught that Christians should only be involved in spiritual things. The world in its material or physical form belongs to Satan and we should have nothing to do with it.

God's way is the polar opposite. Seek first the Kingdom of God and bring that into every sphere of life. Jesus says

> My prayer is not that you take them out of the world but that you protect them from the evil one. They are not of the world, even as I am not of it. Sanctify them by the truth;

> your word is truth. As you sent me into the world, I have
> sent them into the world. (Jn. 17:15–18)

God has sent us into the world. So our nature, our life source, is not of this world, but our sphere of operation and mission very definitely is.

The majority of biblical prophets were working men and women exercising their ministry to the full. They did not have to be paid by the church; in fact that would have been a distinct disadvantage for a whole variety of reasons. Their significance and their contribution were validated and worked out through the job in which God had placed them.

The father of our faith, the prophet and covenant-bearer Abraham, was a travelling farmer and a businessman. Abraham changed his working practice and his way of life to accommodate God's call. Scripture records that Abraham, Isaac and Jacob dwelt in tents. Why record that? Because their work and lifestyle reflected the call of God on their lives. Moses was both an academic and a nomadic farmer in two phases of his life, before becoming an international politician.

Who was the first prophet in the Bible?

I wonder what name came to your mind.

Jesus refers to **the first prophet** as **Abel**. Abel was one of Scripture's first recorded workers, and it was his work-based worship that brought pleasure to the Creator. I have wondered how he could be regarded as a prophet. We have no record of any word he spoke, nor of any scripture produced by him. Somehow, through his worshipful, positive and sacrificial attitudes at work he declared the nature, character and beauty of God.

Joseph's prophetic ministry began in animal husbandry and took him into service in military households, prison management, and finally the highest government office.

Ruth fulfilled the purposes of God as a widow, as a refugee and as a housewife.

Esther changed the course of world history by auditioning as a beauty queen!

Daniel's great revelation concerning the end times was brought to birth as he worked in the civil service and the king's court. His government job included heading up what was essentially a think-tank, developing government policy and providing counsel.

David was a shepherd, poet, musician, military strategist, ruler and harem manager!

Amos ran a flock and a fig grove.

Isaiah was in the king's court.

Zephaniah was a socialite in court service, with political interest.

Ezekiel came from a priestly family yet was incredibly well versed in international affairs, culture, shipbuilding and literature.

Nehemiah was a civil service governor.

Obadiah was head of palace management.

Elisha was a wealthy landowner with the equivalent of twelve combine-harvesters!

I think it's clear that prophecy and work are stablemates. They go together.

What fascinates me is that commentators on prophecy in church history will tell you that one of the reasons for the demise of the early church's prophetic ministry was that travelling prophets expected money from the congregations they visited. In other words, they failed precisely because they let go of the world of work.

At the heart of this problem is a heresy – the belief in a sacred/secular divide.

We deal with this in detail in the book *Love Work, Live Life!* But the idea that work is secular is a pagan Greek concept, a masterpiece of demonic deception that has permeated church thinking and practice. It has prevented God's people from seeing all they could be and do. It brainwashes us into believing that church work and the working world are two different worlds. One is inherently spiritual, godly and always impacting eternity, the other one is not. My working world then becomes a necessary evil. I do it, but at the same time I'm trying desperately to release my time and energy and future into something which my brainwashing tells me is more spiritual and more valuable. This can produce big tensions, setting up competing demands from what we wrongly interpret as two opposing worlds. It can cause confusion in our minds and is very likely to stop God's people using their gifts in the workplace, because they have never been taught that is where we can and should function with those gifts.

Did you know that for every time Jesus operated in the gifts of the Spirit in a place of worship, he operated outside of that context five or six times?

God does not see things in this way

In my study at home I have a piece of stone. It's not very impressive to look at or feel. But it came from one of the most famous walls in history. This stone – if it could talk – would tell you stories of incredible suffering and anguish. It could tell you of a woman smuggled through in a hi-fi until her baby cried and she was shot by the East European guards. It could tell you about a young man who was about to make it all the way over the wall when he too was shot, and as he lay dying, the guards on the western side could only throw him medical supplies. This wall could tell you about millions of people separated from their loved ones.

But it could also tell you that one day, a tiny breach was made in it, and that before long something that had taken years to construct came tumbling down and the world was changed for ever. Of course that was preceded by talking, dialogue, a message of hope. Teachers, prophets, parents, leaders and politicians all had their place in sharing that message of hope, until that message became a movement which quickly saw the wall of division collapse and a new freedom emerge.

The wall, of course, was the Berlin wall, once the scene of sad and heroic stories which still inspire to this day.

You and I can quickly grasp the devil's masterpiece of deception, because if he can convince Christians that work is secular and so called Christian work is sacred, then every thinking child of God spends their life wishing they were doing something more spiritual than they are doing now. But as we go through this material, that wall can come crumbling down.

Dreaming about work

God wants to see our prophetic gift released in every dimension of our lives, and that includes the workplace. I saw it like this in a dream: I dreamt of soldiers, dressed and equipped for battle, strong and healthy. But then I saw battalion after battalion, tens of thousands of troops, far away from the front line, far away from the real battle. I asked, why aren't these soldiers fighting in the front line? Then a voice replied, 'It's because no one has told them they are front-line troops.'

Listen: whatever sphere of work God has led you to, you are one of his front-line troops. See it. Believe it. Let God release you to fulfil the purpose he has for you, right where you are.

The prophet–king relationship

When a person acquires power, in whatever form or sphere, some people will be attracted to them, while others will keep at a distance.

Those who congregate around the powerful leader may well be circumspect when it comes to voicing opinions that are not the current fashion. Those who are far off will not move in the right circles to be heard anyway. Given this tendency, the leader can easily become isolated and end up not knowing who their real friends are.

So the question arises: who is prepared to speak truthfully to the leader?

In ancient times, kings and queens had absolute power – not always a good thing. In this context, prophets played an important role. Prophets held a plumb line to the leader's behaviour, and when it departed from what was good and just and wise, the prophet would confront the issue. This confrontation often took the form of a vision in which the consequences of the behaviour were graphically demonstrated.

Today, wise leaders need their true friends to have a prophetic role. I often hear leaders say, 'Who is it that I can really trust in my organisation to talk to me truthfully?'

One of my good friends runs a leadership masterclass with senior leaders in the Ministry of Defence. The facilitators help them to look at how to define that which is true, and how to detect activity that's off your radar. My friend introduced into this the concept of the prophet and king.

Working from some material written by Charles Handy, he pointed out that every king needs a prophet: someone who is prepared to tell you the truth without fear or favour and to tell it to you as they really see it.

At one point, a government minister was brought in. Those who had been in the training session explained the concept and then asked the minister, who are your prophets?

The minister waffled for some time before he caught himself and said with remarkable honesty, 'You can tell by the answer to my question I don't have prophets around me or those who are prepared to tell me how it really is; what I have is a lot of people saying what they think I would like to hear. A lot of people with brown noses, following their own ambitions and careers. The result? I feel isolated and disconnected. Looking at my answer, I am actually concerned and scared that I have no one around me who is prepared to tell me the truth.'

Prophets call out for integrity and righteousness.

One of my favourite clients for many years was Nick Robinson, Chairman of the Marketing Guild. Whenever he introduced me, he introduced me as 'the company conscience'. I treasured that title more than any other I have been given, because he understood and welcomed the fact that I was free to challenge the Guild on issues of integrity and ethical marketing.

So it is that prophets put in positions by God hold leaders to account and point to the consequences of their attitudes and actions. A good question to ask if you are a prophet who has this kind of capacity is, who are the kings I can serve?

If you are a leader in the workplace or the church, you might want to ask yourself, do I have such prophets around me?

Prophetic words at work

I remember going out to lunch after a sales visit – being driven in a prospect's Rolls-Royce and feeling a little intimidated. As we sat down to a splendid meal, I felt the sense that this man had some real sadness in his family. I still felt somewhat intimidated, so I put it to him something like this: 'I think you have some pain in your family, don't you – would you like to tell me about it?' This wealthy man's eyes brimmed with tears and he began to share about his disabled daughter. That conversation led into a time of sharing and a relationship that lasted for many years.

One of my friends, Andy Forbes, is a church pastor, but he will say that almost without exception the life-changing prophetic words and dreams he has had have been in the workplace or the community. On one occasion, Andy was waiting for a train to take him from Croydon to Central London. On the platform was a tall black man standing among several hundred waiting passengers. Andy felt the Spirit say to him, 'Tell that man I love him.' Andy was understandably reluctant, and walked up the platform to a place where no one was standing, to be alone. The man suddenly and quite deliberately moved up the platform and stood next to Andy. Andy had to laugh, and told the man what he felt God had said. They got into the carriage together and by the end of that journey the man had given his life to Christ. As he finished the train journey he turned to Andy and said, 'My mother's a Christian and has been praying for me for years.'

I know of someone else who uses her prophetic insight in business consultancy. One client was being extremely awkward and obstructive to the work in hand. Ruth turned to this man and said, 'I get the feeling you would have liked to rebel as a teenager, but your mother wouldn't let you.' A risky thing to do in business, but she was right on target and facilitated change in the individual.

An important point to make here is that my friend doesn't go looking to act prophetically. Prophetic people are often not even aware that they are operating in their gift; it's almost second nature.

Prophets and workplace motivation

Prophetic people communicate in a way which builds up and motivates. They are responsible for equipping people for works of service, which invariably involves helping people to discover who they are and what gifting they have.

In my working arena I run seminars around the world on practical business principles for success. We have business training, CDs, in-house training and large-scale national and international business seminars and events (details at the end of the book). I am so blessed and fulfilled in doing this, and for me it is a seamless extension of my prophetic gifting. God has opened up some amazing opportunities for our team, including addressing thousands of business leaders around the world on work-life balance and the place of family life.

Our company runs events on sales, marketing, negotiation and leadership. The concepts and principles we endeavour to work from are biblically rooted. But we are not overt with references to the Bible or Christianity. It's not uncommon to have people come up and engage on a distinctly spiritual level. I remember one delegate who came up after a high-intensity sales seminar and said, 'This has not been about selling, it's been about life.'

On another occasion, when I was running an event at the Institute of Directors on marketing, a business owner asked if we could have a chat. We stopped for a coffee, and this successful lady began to tell me all about her excellent little business. But as she did so, a strange thing happened, and it's happened to me a number of times. She began to pour out her life story, and said through her tears, 'I don't know why I am doing this.' Behind those tear-filled eyes was a brain that held the database of her top one hundred clients – she even knew their children's names – but something was happening to her. She was instinctively asking, can I make it in business and have a life? Somehow the invisible but real prophetic dimension in the seminar and in the coffee shop was touching a life. All this is an extension of being prophetic in the workplace.

Prophets and strategy

The first book of Chronicles talks about the prophet bringing practical solutions for success. In today's language you might call that strategy. It is fascinating to see how interested and willing to be involved God is, when it comes to our workplace. Let me illustrate from the working world of one of my close friends.

Andy works for a multinational organisation with responsibility for Europe, the Middle East and Africa. I choose Andy's stories because he is one who regularly sees solutions from God for problems in his workplace setting.

Andy writes:

I was running a business unit (in excess of £100 million turn-over per year) and facing some complex technology changes in my industry. Firstly, I had a real sense from God that changes were happening that would influence my market and that a response was needed by me. I also had a clear vision of what I needed to do to be ready for that change. It meant I would have to completely reshuffle my management team and the staff underneath them. This last part was very complex and for two weeks I theorised seemingly every option, but was stuck. Then one morning, God gave me a picture. It was a full-colour vision of an organisational chart with the names of all the people in place. I hurriedly wrote the organisational chart onto a big whiteboard. It was clear, simple and brilliant. It worked, and the outcome was a very successful financial year as a result of the reorganisation.

I regularly see numbers, sometimes whole spreadsheets, in my mind. I am able to see what is happening behind the numbers. This helps me to quickly recommend improvements. For example, I was able to 'see' some specific stock levels on certain products that were excessively high, and this needed fast action. When the inventory level was physically checked, what I had 'seen' was correct. I often see business plans and marketing campaigns in my mind. This saves hours of time and often the resulting ideas are incredibly effective. As a result of this I was able to win an industry award three years in a row in recognition of my achievements.

Seers at work

A friend of mine was working with a colleague who is a real 'seer' into people's personal situations. The work involved facilitating a very senior group of people in the public sector, who were working to develop their strategic plans. Almost a day into a two-day event, the group were totally blocked and were not making any progress. There was a strong feeling of being disempowered and there was little enthusiasm for the strategic work. My friend and his colleague had run out of ideas, so they decided to take a break. As he was washing his hands in the bathroom my friend's eye caught a sign which said in large letters DON'T LEAVE TAPS RUNNING. Then he noticed another sign: PULL THE CHAIN. Then another: PUT ALL LITTER IN THE BIN. At that moment he knew the reason why they were struggling with this group. He came out into the corridor and met his colleague. 'Did you know there are eleven signs in the men's toilet?' he said. To which she responded, 'There are thirteen of them in the ladies.'

They returned to the meeting and declared, 'We've just seen something in the toilet that explains how you are feeling.' Of course, the group thought they had completely lost the plot. But they marched everyone down to the toilets and asked them, 'What do you see?' Their initial answers are not really repeatable, but eventually they too saw what my friends were getting at. All the notices were negative: don't do this, don't do that. Then they took them to the entrance foyer. There was no welcome, only more negative notices. In the lift, more of the same; down the corridors, more of the same. In fact the whole building was riddled with signs telling people what to do and what not to do.

The penny finally dropped. No wonder they felt disempowered. What an atmosphere to work in. What a negative statement about who they were and what they valued. Since they were senior management, they took the decision to remove all the signs and where necessary replace them with more positive ones. They placed flowers and a large welcome sign in the foyer. Only then did my friends return to the task at hand, the strategic review.

Our generation is surely crying out for reformers in health care, in education, in the justice system and in law and order. Great prophetic voices from the past, such as William Wilberforce, William Booth and the education reformer Robert Raikes, stir the heart and mind. There is a huge need in our day for young men and women to see the prophetic possibilities in areas such as fair trading, abortion, education, medical ethics, human trafficking and globalisation. For church leaders, my encouragement would be to keep these fields of opportunity in front of your young people as they consider what to do with their lives.

Sometimes it's helpful to see a progression, to help us slide into some of the wider applications God has for us.

Family

In general terms, God has chosen the family as a way to make himself known. The family is a marvellous base for learning to bring the prophetic word in a secure environment. In one family that I know, the father was preparing to meet a church member with two elders. The elders had concerns that the church member was deceiving them in all kinds of ways, especially with his story of conversion. As the family was having a meal together, the father asked if anyone had a word that they would like to share. After a short while, one of the children spoke: 'There is a boat; you and the elders are in the boat. There is a man not in the boat but in the water. He thinks he is in the boat but he is not. After a while a wave will come and bring the man to the boat.'

From the mouth of a pre-teen came great wisdom for the elders dealing with what was in fact quite a difficult issue.

Church

We have looked at this in some detail, but bringing the prophetic into the church is at the next level of learning and experience. Practice and adjustment here will serve us well for our wider roles.

Work and vocation

We have looked at some biblical examples. Joseph, for example, was involved in strategy, God's direct word, direction and dreams. Esther was able to operate creative strategies without mentioning the name of God. Daniel worked in the inner circles of highest-level government. He handled occult team members and brought supernatural revelation and inspired thinking and planning to the rulers of his day. We have looked together at some practical examples.

Wider issues in society

In the last twenty years we have seen some attempts to branch out and act prophetically in aspects of public life.

1. Morality

Joanna Thompson of CARE Centres Network tells her story:

I had been a Christian for just over ten years and I attended a lively church. However, I felt restless. In fact I became quite a nuisance to those around me. I think in exasperation my pastor asked me what I really wanted to do. Looking back, I believe that question unlocked what God had put in my heart. I wanted to be involved with those who didn't know Jesus. I had tripped over God's mercy and love and there was a deep longing in me to see others experience his grace.

I wanted to do something outside the church and to put my faith into practice in the community where I lived. I'm not a talker, so I never dreamt I could counsel, but God had other plans. We only thought of reaching out to women in crisis on a local basis, but very soon we were receiving requests from other churches around the country to come and help them set up centres. I loved speaking about this work, which was now so close to my heart. The first time I spoke publicly I remember feeling 'I am made for this!'

Twenty years on there are 160 centres in the UK as well as many overseas which are affiliated to the network we established. We also run a national free phone helpline CAREconfidential (0800 028 2228) and provide confidential on-line support through www.careconfidential.com. Literally thousands of children are alive today because their mothers came to a centre or contacted CAREconfidential. Women who have had abortions have found healing and peace and many have come to know the love of God, no matter what their circumstances. God's plans and desires are so much bigger than ours.

2. Education

School governors are the unpaid men and women who run our schools. A number of Christian people are serving as school governors. Christian education for non-churched children is a message that people are acting on and thinking through right now. Some academies have seen this put into place.

3. The poor

I read about a church in Cincinnati which fed more poor in one year than the local government department responsible. In the end the government department came and asked the church to run the whole city programme.

Churches throughout the UK reach out to the poor in their own communities with the love and compassion of Jesus.

Tony Campolo is famous for his 'Prostitutes' birthday party' and 'The church that holds parties for prostitutes'.

These are all prophetic initiatives, mainly tactical in application. But there are other, more far-reaching attempts. Make Poverty History has achieved some great results. In 2005 the world saw Nelson Mandela address over 20,000 people in Trafalgar Square, 25,000 people take part in the Trade Justice vigil and a phenomenal 250,000 people take to the streets of Edinburgh, demanding that world leaders make poverty history. Whatever our personal views about these initiatives, they are good examples of prophetic activity with global reach.

4. Stewardship

A man called John Smith in British Columbia, Canada, got depressed and was in despair over the destruction of the forests. Someone faced him with this question: 'Whose trees are these?' He went back to his forestry with renewed vigour and instigated a programme called the Silver Culture Programme, in which he blended harvest and replant, and discovered a new method of logging silver spruce that saved the trees. That programme now runs through the whole of British Columbia.

5. Local, national and international government

This area is now receiving a lot of attention. Of the 650 MPs in the House of Commons, 120 meet for prayer. In the USA both President and Secretary of State talk openly about their faith.

The point I want to make in looking at these areas of life is that often there is a progression from family to church, to work life, to major issues or government responsibilities. In the light of what you have read in this chapter, I would encourage you to seek God and be willing to be stirred to use your gifting with fresh horizons and creativity. May God take the blinkers off any sense of parochial operating of these gifts and give you eyes to see way beyond where you are today.

We are experiencing massive religious, political, technological, biological and economic changes, with consequences we can only guess at. I suspect, despite the illusion of certainty and progress offered by the guru's crystal ball, most of us in the working world feel we are on a roller coaster ride, never quite sure which way is up. What a time for us as Christians to be salt and light; what a time to see a prophetic voice bringing some of God's certainties.

Summary

- The gift of prophecy is for the workplace as much as the church meeting
- The prophets of Scripture used their gift in the workplace
- Don't believe the sacred/secular divide
- We need prophets to hold the 'kings' of leadership in different spheres to account
- Prophets at work motivate, form strategy and see solutions
- The prophetic progresses from family to church, to work, to nations

12

The Calling of the Prophet

We have a dangerous tendency in the evangelical and charismatic church to think primarily of 'church' when we consider calling. It's understandable, because most of our heroes and role models within the last ten to twenty years have primarily been so called 'full-time' pastors, 'full-time' church-based teachers, 'full-time' evangelists and even 'full-time' prophets.

Those who have preached calling and envisioned us have in the main been church-employed ministries. Now, God-given as all these ministries are, it leaves us with a filter that says, 'I am fully approved by God only when my gifting is expressed to the full within the church context.'

Nothing could be further from the truth!

Of course the church is desperate for the prophetic word, and of course prophetic ministry must be released to flourish, but it must never stop there. The church is not to be a parasite, sucking into itself all the most able, the most gifted, the most prophetic. The Ephesians 4 ministries exist to equip the people of the church and to fling them out into every available sphere of Spirit-led activity.

I am still waiting for full-time pastors and leadership teams to see their best young men and women and groom them for a role in the working world or the community. As I see it, the primary responsibility of leadership teams in the church is to cause God's people to discover and fulfil their destiny, their part in God's kingdom on earth.

For the majority of Christians, our main sphere of calling and destiny will not be the church. If we think about it for any length of time, this should be fairly obvious. After all, if our church has one hundred members, there may be four or five key functions at most. Probably only one or two of those will be paid by the church. If deep down I believe that I should be full-time or believe that only full-time work in the church is truly valuable, truly spiritual and truly worthwhile, I will live a restricted lifestyle and never see the full power or potential of God released. Two, three or even more meetings per week will never provide the environment where I can fully express all the marvellous provision of God the Holy Spirit within me, nor will they facilitate the responsibility I have to know and function in my calling.

So many men and women with a prophetic gift and calling have been robbed of the prophetic power of God in their workplace because they have been indoctrinated to think, feel and believe that their work is second-best, secular, an occupation to pay for their contribution to the church.

God's people need envisioning to believe in their scriptural sending into the world and all the potential that awaits them in it. Work, in any and every sphere, is service, is spiritual and is ministry if we let God in.

Ephesians 4 tells us that the purpose of the ministry gifts is to equip us for works of service. Those works will invariably be outside the church.

The process of God's calling

It is easy to have an unhelpful expectation of what God's calling may or may not be. We may have been taught just one side of calling and missed the other. The New Testament word for calling is *klesis* – an invitation, calling or summons.

As far as the New Testament is concerned we are all called. The Greek for church is *ekklesia*, meaning 'the called out ones'.

God's people often have an unhealthy preoccupation with this so-called calling. Calling as a word in the New Testament is not at all limited to the narrow sense of personal destiny, which is the main meaning we seem to give it. As we shall see, everyone is called, and the discovery of that calling lies within us.

Calling happens in different ways to very different types of people.

Different types of calling

Joseph was spoken to by God in a dream.

Elisha was called by another man – Elijah.

Jeremiah was set apart before he was even born – as was John the Baptist.

Isaiah was already prophesying when a seraph touched his lips with a live coal and he was commissioned for a specific task.

Samuel heard God's audible voice calling him.

Daniel's ministry started not with a divine encounter but with a refusal to eat foods!

Zechariah simply wrote down what he saw – and God took it and used it.

Haggai similarly wrote down what God gave him: God took it and used it.

Elijah seems to just 'appear' in Scripture, operating in his gifting without any record of a specific calling or previous supernatural encounter.

Different social backgrounds

Joseph – a shepherd.

Zephaniah – a member of the royal family.

Samuel – an adopted son.

Jeremiah – a priest.

Daniel – a courtier.

Elisha – a wealthy landowner.

Jeremiah – a single man with few friends.

Called at a wide range of ages

Jeremiah – before he was born!

Samuel – 12 years old.

Joseph – 17 years of age.

Zechariah – a young man.

Haggai – in his early 70s.

One important lesson we can learn from this is that our age, our family background and social standing are immaterial. The list shows people of all kinds being called, and at different stages of life, from babies to old men, from wealthy landowners to prisoners and lowly shepherds.

You can see this illustrated in the Christmas story. Who is it that God chooses to speak to regarding the birth of his beloved son? High-income travelling consultants (magi) and low-income, working-class shepherds. The two ends of the scale in terms of socio-economic grouping – yet God brings them together under one roof.

What can we summarise from all this? God's marvellous and varied nature will never be restricted to one method, one mode, one manifestation. God may speak to us before we're born, when we are 12, when we are 17, when we are in our twenties to thirties, or when we are 70! He may speak to us in a dream, in an appearance, through angels, with an audible voice, through another's ministry.

A calling by encounter

In my early twenties I worked with Youth With A Mission in Tanzania and Kenya. At some point the team was out in the bush and I got an inner ear infection. I kept a diary at that time and I know that the infection lasted for forty days. It was in one ear, then in the other, and finally in both. The pain was acute, and with no drugs available I was in a bad state. The only thing that stayed with me out of that time was a scripture: 'He who has an ear, let him hear what the Spirit says to the churches' (Rev. 2:7).

Some weeks later I travelled down to Zimbabwe and fell sick again, this time with malaria and dysentery. During my convalescence I was staying at the home of two carers. One morning I walked into the study. On the floor a book was lying open, and at the top of the page was a new chapter heading with that very scripture underneath it.

At the time I had no clue what it meant or what its importance was. I had probably only encountered one or two prophetic words in my entire life. It was four or five years later, in a period when I was being discipled, that the penny dropped. Five years later that calling transformed my focus, my life and my capacity. It was as if, because I saw it, I wanted to take responsibility for it, nurture and develop it, and pay almost any price for it.

My close friend and co-worker John Denning was a farmer and a shepherd in rural Hampshire. John wasn't really aware of the prophetic except from stories of Old Testament prophets. When he was baptised in the Spirit, God began to speak to him immediately. In 1969 the Lord spoke to him in a cave in Torquay:

If you utter worthy, not worthless, words, you will be my
spokesman. (Jer. 15:19)

John realised that God had spoken to him, but was not
aware that this was a call to the prophetic. In fact, the
preceding words in Jeremiah have to do with repentance,
so John's first thought was that this was somehow God
endeavouring to discipline him. Twenty-four hours later
John sensed the Lord saying, 'I'm calling you up.' In other
words, I'm not calling you to repentance on this occasion;
I'm calling you up to utter worthy words. For John – just as
it as was for me – even then the penny simply did not drop.
It was not until 1977, eight years later, that a leader came
to John and said, 'You are like a mystic, like a prophet.' It
was at that point that John realised the calling was to be
prophetic.

In 1981 the Lord came as a vision in the night. John
woke, aware that somebody was in the room. He couldn't
see the person, but he could hear the voice. As John sat
bolt upright, he heard these words: 'I want you to read
Amos.' That was it, no more and no less. John wrestled
with the meaning of this. He read and reread Amos but
it was almost twenty years before the significance of this
dawned. In chapter 7 Amos says, 'I was a shepherd and I
also took care of sycamore-fig trees.' John is a shepherd-
prophet, but it took him decades from the divine encounter
to perceive it.

Of all the prophetic people I know, there is no one like
John, who with his wife Marilyn cares for the flock of God
in pastoral ways. Few prophets can do it. John's divine
encounter and his faithfulness in using his gifts have
enabled him to walk that journey.

It's fascinating, isn't it, that even with a supernatural
encounter it can be years before we grasp what God is
saying. Equally interesting is that for both John and me

it took other leaders speaking affirmation into our lives to release that gifting. I do believe that there are some reading this who have had dreams, encounters, visitations or words, and some of us have forgotten, buried or by-passed those words. You say to me, 'Surely I couldn't mislay, forget or bury such an encounter?' My experience is that you certainly can.

As you read, I pray that right now, at this moment, there would be a release of memory, a blowing away of the leaves that have covered the call of God on your life – where the enemy has 'snatched' the seeds of God's encounter.

The calling is in the gift

The majority of us, as with the majority of those in Scripture, simply don't get a divine encounter. Some feel second-rate or second-division as a result. But it doesn't work like that in the eyes of God. The reason is that the calling is in the gift itself. The gift is an invitation, a summons to work with God the Holy Spirit. The lack of some other divine encounter is not even necessarily a measure of the scope, the scale or the dimension of our gifting. The lack of some extra divine encounter should never stop us working out our gift for all we are worth. The gifting itself is enough. As we lay down our lives to steward that gift, God as it were switches on a divine autopilot that opens ever-increasing horizons of destiny – just faithfully putting to work what we have will work out our call.

For some, God will speak a calling into being, and we will find our gifts getting behind that spoken word, enabling us to fulfil it. For others (the majority), as we apply ourselves and use our gifts, they will open up the destiny that was written into our beings at conception.

The fabulous truth is that God has written our calling and destiny into our spiritual genetics, our spiritual DNA. New birth unlocks its potential.

Sometimes a divine encounter will precede its fulfilment and direct its path. At other times, faithfully using the gift and laying down our life to fulfil our responsibility – as Daniel did – will open our eyes and direct our path, and we will find ourselves drawn by the Holy Spirit to outwork God's call on our lives.

If you're one of those who already have a divine encounter related to your calling, then get behind it with all your heart, soul, mind and body and seek God for its fulfilment.

If, like the majority of Christians, we don't have some specific or dramatic divine encounter, let's take the encounter provided in the gifts themselves and let's work at that with all our heart, soul, mind and body – leaving the sphere or the breadth of our calling to God himself. Let's allow it to unfold before us.

The Scripture links gifts and callings. Paul says in Romans 11:29 that the gifts and call of God are irrevocable. We can put it another way and say that the gift itself is a calling, a summons, an invitation – and that calling is to use the gift. God will never give us gifts that he has not called us to use. The Holy Spirit is a wellspring of life, a well that contains water of destiny and calling. Using the gift – not waiting for an encounter – is what determines our future and what unlocks our destiny.

Care for the Family regularly runs events based on the material in *Love Work, Live Life!* At those events we ask the question, 'How many of you would like to know the will or purpose of God for your life?' We can rely on a staggering response. At nearly every event 80 per cent raise their hands. In fact more than 80 per cent of the average congregation have no idea of their calling. My cry, my passion is that each and every member would discover and use their gifts – then their callings would surely emerge.

Leaders, we have probably encouraged our people to be waiting for some dramatic encounter with God because that's what we were taught. But the vast majority of God's people, including his prophets, simply need to be encouraged to see what they have already received, and encouraged to lay down their lives in order to steward that. The truth is that the Body of Christ will not grow until each member does its part.

Whatever your job or field of service, and in a sense regardless of it, you are a called person. Os Guinness puts it this way:

> The truth is, God calls us to himself so decisively that every-thing we are, everything we do, and everything we have is invested with a special devotion and dynamism lived out as a response to his summons and service.

So whatever our job or occupation, our calling is to serve God here and now through it, because of it, and not despite it. We are to serve God and love our neighbour, to love God and do good to others through our gift.

Call and gifting are not our choice

We can, and will, ask for gifts of the Holy Spirit – and we are encouraged to do just that. However, God has his own plan, his own timetable, his own unique selection of gifts which are tailor-made for us and his purpose that he wants to fulfil through us.

There is a well-known passage in the Psalms:

> You knit me together in my mother's womb ... When I was woven together in the depths of the earth, your eyes

saw my unformed body. All the days ordained for me were written in your book before one of them came to be. (Ps. 139:13, 15–16)

We have natural genetics. That means we can't choose our skin colour, our eye colour, our race, or even whether we will be male or female. In the same way, we have spiritual DNA, which determines the gifts and callings and purposes of God. We have some ordained days to walk in.

For we are God's workmanship, created in Christ Jesus to do good works, which God prepared in advance for us to do. (Eph. 2:10)

How do we find these ordained days, these good works created before we were born? Easy! Put the gifts within you to work, and see those days and good works appear.

We can resist a calling

Another reason why God may have given us the book of Jonah is to show us how easy it is to resist a calling. There are a number of prophetic people who are pain-averse. Jeremiah wants to resist so badly that God commands him to repent. For him, the calling and the word of God were so powerful that resisting gave him internal physical pain.

We can resist by wanting to be someone else, to have their ministry, their impact, their blessing. This is a form of covetousness. Whatever drives us to want to be different to the way God has crafted us – insecurity, pride, covetousness – needs to be settled. Discovering who we are not is as valuable as discovering who we are. Being content and secure in who we are is a great asset and a source of release for the gift within us.

We can presume a calling

At the other end of the scale, pride, insecurity or comparing ourselves with others can cause us to presume gifts and callings that are just not there. Sometimes an appointment to a position assumes certain gifts which we do not have. I was once asked to take on the job of pastoring a church in a nearby town. The reality was twofold. On one level, in my pride I thought I could do the job with ease. I was in a fairly responsible commercial management role at the same time, and I really thought I could handle both. The problem was that I am simply not equipped to be a pastoral person and the load crushed me within a year or so. I had a burnout and physical exhaustion, and twenty years later I still carry some of the scars from that experience. One outcome of that was the realisation that I am not a person with pastoral gifting, nor am I equipped to handle people's problems day after day: I find it crushing. I presumed a calling which nearly broke me.

The confirmation of our calling by others

Another factor in determining the authenticity of a calling is the observations of others. If others do not affirm the gift that I think I have, then the likelihood is I do not have that gift or calling. If my work in God does not produce the fruit that should accompany my gifting, then I don't have it and I should face that fact with releasing joy. For example, if I think I have the gift of an evangelist but almost no one gets saved through me, then I have to question whether I do actually have that gift. If I think I am a pastor and great at counselling, but no one comes back for more, or if no one says thanks, that really changed my life and set me free, then I almost certainly don't have that calling or that gift. Simple to write but painful to experience, I know!

Summary

- Most of us will experience our call outside the church setting
- We are all called in one way or another
- There are different ways of being called
- The calling is in the gift
- We cannot choose our gift and call
- But we can resist it!

13

The Prophet's Character

Whether your call came by divine encounter or through the gifts of the Spirit within, the call and the sending will not be at the same time. Often the two are separated by decades, and certainly by years. We don't look for harvest at the time we are sowing seed.

One of the main reasons for this process is the question of character. Our life experience and age at the time of our calling mean our character needs adjustment. Let me illustrate. Joseph gets an amazing dream, rich in destiny. For him it is crystal clear. In presumption he shares it unwisely with his brothers and father. That presumption reveals his pride and he is off on a roller coaster ride to prepare him for that destiny. After seeing a mighty vision, he gets thrown into a pit by his brothers. He is sold into slavery, then put into prison. In the process he is exposed to unkindness from his family, false accusation and wrong imprisonment before he finally stands before Pharaoh. He had thirteen years of these dealings and a further seven years before his dream was fulfilled. That's twenty years between the calling by divine encounter and the sending or fulfilment of that encounter.

Moses is described as a man with a unique face-to-face relationship with God. He receives his calling, then murders an Egyptian in his eagerness to be God's man of power. Moses had experienced the most luxurious lifestyle in the world at the time. He had a brilliant education, probably walked past Cleopatra's needle en route to school every day, and would have had access to the technology that built the pyramids. But then he has to run from all of that to the desert for forty years. Forty years of very hot, boring, sheep-minding. Forty years working in searing heat in relatively primitive surroundings, before he has another divine encounter in the form of the burning bush, and shortly afterwards is nearly killed by God himself. Now, at the age of 80, he begins to work out that calling and embarks on the tough work of leading the children of Israel out of their captivity. Only after another forty years of leadership and national military campaigns does he become known as the meekest man on the face of the earth.

What about David? Before he kills Goliath, it is recorded that he kills a lion and bear. He spends years as a fugitive, a hunted outlaw, even though he has been anointed publicly by Samuel. And yet in all of that he learns to love and respect the existing authority of Saul and his kingdom – learning to call his enemy 'father'. It was forty years from his anointing before he was the king of all Israel.

Why does it need this process?

The calling and the gifts produce a desire, but do not give the necessary ability, proven character or maturity. Calling and gifting usually expose what is actually in us. Pride surfaces, together with a whole host of other things. Often there can be a presumption that we hear from God and speak from God, when in reality we can't yet tell the difference between what come from our own flesh, our own strength, and what comes from God. These things take years to learn.

God wants to bring us to maturity, the kind of maturity that is totally dependent on his strength and knows our own weakness. Only when the reality of our own weakness dawns can we be truly ready to be used by God.

Watchman Nee in *The Normal Christian Life* puts it this way:

> God must bring us to a point – I cannot tell you how it will be, but He will do it – where, through a deep and dark experience, our natural power is touched and fundamentally weakened, so that we no longer dare trust ourselves. He has had to deal with some of us very strangely, and take us through difficult and painful ways, in order to get us there. At length there comes a time when we no longer 'like' to do Christian work – indeed we almost dread to do things in the Lord's Name. But then at last it is that He can begin to use us ...
>
> Every true servant of God must know at some time that disabling from which he can never recover; he can never be quite the same again. There must be that established in you which means that from henceforth you will *really* fear yourself. You will fear to move out on the impulse of your soul, for you know what a bad time you will have in your own heart before the Lord if you do ... and your response to the Father of our spirits is: 'Abba, Father.'

I remember the penny dropping more clearly for me when I saw the epic film *The Ten Commandments*. When Moses is banished to the desert, the narrator declares: 'God purges his messengers until they are ground into dust from whence they came – then they are reeds (supple and pliable); they can bend whichever way he wills.'

Proven character is normally a prerequisite to fulfilling the callings of God. And it seems that most, if not all, of the men and women of God in Scripture followed the same pattern – which gives hope for every one of us. No one individual started off mature or perfect. Each man or woman received their call through their gifts or by divine encounter. That call itself began to expose all kinds of weaknesses and deficiencies. God then set in motion a programme designed to bring their desire into line with their ability.

Erratic and unnerving

The problem with the prophetic gifting is that our temperament can make other people rather uncomfortable.

That dramatic capacity which can have value in expressing a word of God can lead to the drama-queen personality, which others find overbearing, even irritating.

That black-and-white, right-and-wrong, plumb-line temperament can bring wonderful clarity in a word that brings the church up short. However, in day-to-day life and relationships it can produce an unyielding spirit. It's not nice to be around, and it's wearing in relationships.

That willingness to speak the truth at all costs can produce a person who is insensitive and careless in relationships, at work or in church life – someone who can give a prophetic word but who is so sensitive that they find correction or criticism of any sort almost unbearable.

Some have left churches or relationships on the strength of these experiences, whereas with care they could have been matured and developed. We forget so easily that to God, character is far more important than what we call ministry. The irrefutable proof for that is found in the qualities required for elders and deacons in Timothy and Titus. With my limited capacity for maths, I make it thirty-three character tests, against just one ministry test. That is God's view and God's balance.

Every gifting has stereotyped characteristics that may not hold true for everyone, but at least give an idea of how others view that gifting and the potential personality traits.

When asked to present material on this, one friend of mine – an apostle – drew on his own four decades of working with prophets to list the following traits of the prophet:

- Tending to be impatient
- Insensitive
- Discourteous
- Tending to be independent
- Reactionary
- Overly emotional
- Inconsistent, hot and cold
- Tending to have difficulty in relating to church government

I would add insecurity as another very common trait of prophetic personalities.

These are inevitably generalisations, but they can provide an excellent starting point for character development. It's a checklist to kick-start any prophetic discipleship. As a prophet myself I don't find it offensive (I have my own list for apostles and pastors and teachers!). I think this is reality.

And of course, for each of these negative traits there is a powerful wonderful positive:

- Impatience leads to seeking God for a better way. It leads to unwillingness to sit in endless, pointless, leaders' meetings. It leads to getting something done

- Insensitive means this man or woman can deliver a word even when it may cost them or embarrass them
- Discourteous means they will not normally be overawed by political correctness or by a person's position
- Independent can mean they are willing to go against the flow and are willing to challenge even the strongest of leaders
- Reactionary means at least someone does react – challenging issues can be embraced
- Emotional means they can communicate the tears, the love, the anger and the peace of God
- Inconsistent means they can communicate at times with enormous passion, the kind of passion that leads to conviction and change
- Difficulty with relating to church government means they are not afraid to confront at any level and can bring an objective voice of truth when others would be afraid to
- Insecurity means I have to push into God, I have to depend upon God, and I can readily understand my own weakness and limitations

The thing is, if as a prophetic person I can have my character developed so that people find it easier to receive from me, and leaders find it easier to trust me, that serves the purposes of God well. If my character cannot be developed or adjusted, then my gift is self-limiting. The possibility of others hearing God through me has been limited by my inability or unwillingness to be changed. The next question, then, is how can we see positive character development?

How does God choose to shape the prophet's character?

I was on a sailing holiday recently when Cheryl-Ann, my youngest daughter, said to me, 'Daisy is such a lovely person, isn't she?' Daisy is our first granddaughter, just five years old. And she is lovely – all four of our grandchildren are. Like all the others she has her moments, but she is lovely and I found myself reflecting on why that was so.

Three areas sprang to mind. Her conception and birth were full of very difficult circumstances and for that reason there is a particular grace of God on her life. Her own make-up and genetics will obviously have something to do with it. And most importantly, the way her parents have carefully, lovingly and with discipline shaped and moulded her has had a huge impact.

1. Circumstances
James 1:2–5 puts it like this:

> Consider it pure joy, my brothers, whenever you face trials of many kinds, because you know that the testing of your faith develops perseverance. Perseverance must finish its work so that you may be mature and complete, not lacking anything. If any of you lacks wisdom, he should ask God, who gives generously to all without finding fault, and it will be given to him.

Trials and circumstantial pressures are the norm, not the exception. And for prophetic people, for the reasons we have discussed, by and large they seem to be more extreme. There is a process in this passage. Trials test faith, which in turn develops perseverance, and that perseverance must finish its work if we want to be mature.

Mature prophets carry a sense of security and peace with them, and will find ears that are more willing to listen and leaders that are more comfortable in working with them. I have always seen this passage in James as something like a pressure cooker. It turns up the heat and increases the pressure, and the job gets done in half the time.

J.B. Phillips translates verse 2 of this passage in this way:

> When all kinds of trials and temptations crowd into your lives, my brothers, don't resent them as intruders, but welcome them as friends!

So pressure and circumstantial trials are not intruders; they are inevitable, and for most of us they will continue to increase. God will invariably take us through fire and water, the extremities of our abilities, humility, patience, courage, willingness and submission. As in the process of refining, over a period of time the heat of all these things will cause the dross of impure motives – fear, distrust, unbelief, cynicism, disobedience – to float up to the surface where they can be exposed and then skimmed off.

Circumstances often appear contrary to the word that God has given. Joseph had his dream of great authority, yet in experience he went down into a pit and into prison. Moses, the promised deliverer, had forty years in the desert.

These apparent contradictions in life can cause God's prophetic people to lose it, to forget the word or to bury it. I had one friend who lost a business, lost his house and had long-term illness in his growing family. He had a prophetic calling concerning leadership and other nations, and in the circumstances and pain the word had got lost or buried. Within eighteen months of repenting for that burying, he was part of the leadership team of a very successful, growing church, and he has been involved in travelling internationally since. The circumstances nearly buried the word.

I think of another prophetic friend of mine working under extreme pressures in a high-flying job with an organisation that is renowned for its poor employee relations. This man has been subject to unfair treatment, abusive and bullying bosses and regular times of uncertainty about his future and his income. There have been many weeks where it has seemed just too much, but through it all he has felt the Spirit of God have him stay there and endure. He shares this with his mature friends who stand with him in prayer. He sees the pain and pressure. What I have seen over eighteen months is God opening up areas of his character to be dealt with. I have seen substantial growth in his capacity to carry heavy weight in leadership, and I see a prophetic gift that is far more clear and powerful today than it was two years ago. My friend can't always see it, but the rest of us can. It's his journey of circumstances that still needs his active response, that still needs his friends' support in prayer, but which is producing maturity of character and developing his gift.

Timing often distresses people. We receive a clear word and then wonder why five years later it is still not fulfilled. As we have seen, it is not uncommon for it to take decades. And that delay is part of the circumstantial pressure, which a loving heavenly Father filters into our lives.

The church will often be my crucible. In the context of commitment to the church, my life is exposed; my faults will not be missed. My life is confronted by leadership, teaching, pastoral care and prophecy. In the closeness of real fellowship I cannot escape or retreat from people, house groups, circumstances that I find difficult to handle. God invests his elders and shepherds with authority, and often that authority can cut right across our will, our thoughts and our desires. Those are the inevitable circumstantial pressures of church life and they are part of our character development. In particular, having my words and attitudes weighed by church leaders can be an intensely hot crucible, especially when I disagree. Those interactions, more than most, will open up my motives and weaknesses. How I handle that process will either develop my character or increase my inclination to believe my own PR.

2. *The genetics of my gift*

This phrase involves a bit of licence. What I mean here is that as we put the gift to work it will inevitably form us and mould us. As we hear God, as we read his Word, as we get revelation, it will change us. As we actually put the colour and shape of our gift to work, the experience over time will enrich and change us. It's about putting to work what is already in me, allowing the process to bring its challenges and changes, and from that being rewarded with more. 'More' probably means a wider sphere within which I can operate my gifting, and enough developed character to handle that increase.

3. *Discipline*

When I reflected on my granddaughter Daisy, I thought back over my own life. Yes, the Word of God has changed me, circumstances have changed me, and the Spirit of God has changed me. But I can say the single most significant contributor to change in my life has been Godly men and women who have been willing to disciple me and to ensure that the Word, the Spirit and circumstances produce lasting change.

Men and women of God will disciple you and will bring affirmation, but if they love you they will bring confrontation too. They will hold up your real behaviour and reflect it back, like a mirror, until out of that process change is birthed.

There is no substitute for this and no short cut round it. This is where change really happens. Jesus saw this as the only way in which his gifted disciples could be moulded enough to spread the gospel around the world.

I have a friend, Barbara, who is also a fellow prophet. When she first came to our church she was deeply wounded from some bad treatment, particularly from a previous fellowship. She came with deep scars. Among other things, her experiences had left her desperately insecure, and unsure of her acceptance as a woman with a prophetic gift. She embraced the process of discipleship. It wasn't easy for her, in fact with her insecurity it was an incredibly courageous and risky thing for her to do. She knew she could have been even more damaged. She ran the risk of being rejected again. She, like many other prophetic people, found the process of having her words weighed hard to bear.

When a prophetic person believes they have heard God, to have that adjusted is hard, but when we are insecure it is doubly hard. It calls into question my ability to hear God and raises the possibility of being rejected. It is tough to break through those things. Barbara embraced the process, however, even though actually the pain sometimes was so intense that it would leave her in tears. We sought to encourage, as well as to shape and guide, and gradually, over months, then years, her words increased in their power. The reach of her gift has gone into other countries; she has had words that have shaped meetings with government ministers and countless words for church leaders, and she is part of a team responsible for developing others with prophetic gifting, which she does with great tenderness and skill. She would tell you that the process of discipleship changed her character, developed her gift and opened doors way beyond her expectation. She could have carried on without it, but she would not have seen her insecurities healed, she would not have seen her gifting increase into the clarity and variety which are her hallmarks today. She would have been weaker without it, and so would the church. Her poem below reflects just that:

New shoots

Why did I duck and dive
to try to outmanoeuvre
You, my Father God,
why so apprehensive
to see you come armed with a knife
to prune Your tree,
YOUR property?
... that dreaded thing
was not an instrument of torture
but a healing scalpel
wielded for my good
(if only Lord I'd understood
the pain it brought to YOU
to cut away dead wood),
... yet NOW You say
You see in me NEW shoots appear,
incisions from Your gentle hands
extract such fragrance here ...
AND promise of more growth to come.
Forgive my complaining attitude,
unwillingness to trust my life,
my call,
into Your tender care,
... I bow before YOUR will
and know, my Lord,

the knife is evidence:
it testifies
You love me still!

Summary

- The gap between call and sending builds character
- God wants us to mature
- Prophets can have negative traits
- But these traits can also be a force for good, for prophetic purpose
- God shapes character through circumstances, genetics and discipline

14

Pair Shape

Only once in the whole of the Bible do prophet and pastor appear in the same verse. However, this is one of the most common pairings in practice and it is fraught with difficulties.

One of the problems we have in the western church is when a pastor runs the church and has responsibility for it. I know this is going to be controversial, but that's unbiblical both in terms of the title and as a way of governing a church. It's unbiblical and it will produce unnecessary tensions, particular between the pastor and the prophet.

In reality there is always plurality of leadership in the Bible.

If it is unavoidable to have just one pastor in charge in the short term, it would be a good idea to bring in an apostle to set boundaries and restraints.

In a local or small regional setting, eldership is essential. You can't have just pastors and prophets and be successful. Local church government at every level in Scripture is plural, and it consists of elders. A church that is governed by one such leader is heading for trouble if it has a prophet or two in its make-up. Either it will blow up or the prophets will be forced to shut up. In an ideal situation there should not be a pastor or a prophet on their own. From the earliest days plurality was the divine order and intention.

Let me explain what the tensions are likely to be by setting out some of the possible differences in style and temperament between a pastor and a prophet.

Pastor	Prophet
fearful of change	excited and motivated by change
reduction of the word	can elevate the word
parochial/local/inward	outward-looking
cork in the bottle	wants to unstop everything
can stop the flow of the Spirit	can overemphasise the Spirit
suspicious of prophets	wary of cautious pastors
tends to mother	tends to be uncaring
settles down	stirs up
stability	innovation
defends	attacks
considers	is impulsive
implementer	envisioner
cooperative	uncooperative
preaches for understanding	preaches for conviction and decision
patient	impatient
open-handed	directive
gentle	assertive
measured	extreme
non-threatening	threatening

Now of course these are outrageous stereotypes, but they make for an interesting dialogue! The point with these contrasts is that they show the likely tensions usually at several points, not just one.

What are some of the particular tensions and how can we handle them?

In the world of work and business, if it is to function well, then like mentors like. Bricklayers train apprentice bricklayers, dentists train student dentists. What's more, you would never go to a bricklayer for a problem with your teeth.

Someone with a pastoral gift or ministry can shape character, can bring adjustment and correction, can open and shut doors, can receive and reject, but he cannot fully train and develop the prophetic ministry within that man or woman. This can be a major source of insecurity for the pastor and a major source of frustration for the prophet.

A wise pastor will point his prophetic men and women to others with a prophetic gifting that is more mature, people who can shape and develop them.

Another area of tension can be that pastors see what needs to be stabilised, cared for, nurtured and bound up. Prophets will often see what is wrong, and what needs to change. The two can appear to be in direct contrast or even conflict, but they are two very necessary sides of one coin.

The whole area of interpretation, application and implementation can be a nightmare for the pastoral person, as can the premature, disorderly or inconsistent behaviour of the prophets. These areas are among the most common causes of confusion and tension between prophet and pastor. This is where plurality is important, but it is especially important for the prophets to take responsibility for weighing words from other prophets. If it is an issue with strategic consequences, then let an apostolic individual be involved in weighing it.

One of the most common tensions for the pastor is when something goes wrong prophetically in a meeting. He is usually a sensitive individual and does not want to correct anyone publicly. He knows that prophets are even more sensitive than he is, so he is reluctant to correct even outside the meeting.

There are many areas which can cause a problem, for example:

- An individual brings three or four contributions, each one slightly weaker than the one before

- A prophetic person brings a prophecy in response to a tongue instead of waiting for the interpretation first – that brings confusion or and a sense of unease

- Only 50 per cent or fewer of the prophecies given appear accurate or of God

We have talked about this in detail earlier in the book, but one of the simplest ways to help the pastoral dimension is for the prophets to take responsibility for adjustment and correction of their own kind. This produces great peace and is the best way I know to develop the prophetic individual concerned. If not, the pastor, ideally working with another pastoral person, will develop a relationship with each prophetic individual and together – using the weighing matrix and the leadership matrix in Appendix 2 of this book – they will learn to work it through together.

Prophets and pastors leading a meeting together, especially when relationships are not strong, can be one of the greatest areas of tension. The pastor can be afraid that the prophets will be wild and uncontrolled or presumptuous. The prophets are paranoid that we will miss God or lose his word, or somehow shut him up.

I don't know how it works in your church, but generally we have found it best for any reasonably large gathering to be led by a team, with someone taking overall responsibility and with a couple of prophets alongside supporting.

I am learning to sail larger boats in the ocean, and one of the things I have to learn is navigation: how to calculate exactly where I am, and then to calculate exactly where to go. I can't do those calculations while I am still helming the boat. Someone else has to do that while I make those calculations.

In Basingstoke, with our six churches, we are blessed with a team of pastors who will do just that. They will take responsibility for steering and getting us under way, but they will allow and encourage prophetically gifted folk to change the direction, even to take the wheel from time to time. This can be done in confidence, because there are usually two or more prophets involved. We will talk together and weigh up what we have, and when we contribute or share it is a joint decision. If we get it wrong, which we will still do from time to time, we can be quite honest with the congregation and share it where that is appropriate.

I think teamwork can be at its best in leading gatherings. Pastors can get a meeting stuck in a rut; prophets can be the ones to see where the Spirit wants to take it. Prophets can often be aware of what God wants from a particular gathering. They can see where the people are coming from. Best of all is when the church can benefit from the stability of the pastoral hand and the sharp focus of the prophet's direction.

Prophets helping out

One of the greatest ways a prophetic team can help the pastors is when they are actively willing to pray and seek God for specific issues. We can't turn that on and off like a cash-dispensing machine, but we can pray and we can ask. If God says nothing, then we can say that. But the fact that we offered to pray and seek God is a blessing and an encouragement. As a practical suggestion, make it known that you are willing to pray. Ring up your pastors and tell them that you are praying and have been praying.

Developing a prophetic team with good relationships with the other leaders can be a blessing to a pastor or local leadership team. With such a team in Basingstoke now long established, we have been able to ensure that we have good prophetic representation in each of the six congregations. Using this group, we have been able to serve the pastoral team in a number of ways. We can offer to take a small prophetic group into a cell group, a congregation, or any other setting. Because they know we will take responsibility, the pastors are fairly relaxed. We make certain that we weigh everything, we judge the words and we sift them, so that training takes place, the prophets' gifting is developed and there is safety. We have seen some tremendous things from these groups: church strategy and change identified, individual callings and ministries released, and occasionally sin exposed.

Five things prophets could do to help pastors
1. Serve with your gift
2. Be accountable to the pastoral individual
3. Be accountable to other prophetic men and women
4. Make it easy for others to approach you and to correct you
5. Don't be defensive when accuracy is challenged or questioned

Five things pastors could do for prophets
1. Open doors for them and the word of God that they carry
2. Rigorously challenge them on their time with God and push them into God
3. Encourage them and let them know you do appreciate the gift
4. Understand that accuracy is learned and developed
5. Draw them in rather than pushing them out

Six rules of combat
1. Don't disagree in public if at all possible

2. Both must be free to share exactly what they feel
3. If there is not a good spirit, suspend any confrontational discussion
4. Always pray afterwards
5. Don't allow the prophet to steamroller the pastor
6. Don't allow the pastor to control the prophet

In all of this, the real issue is relationship: honouring each other and the different gifts we each carry, and spending time together.

But best and safest of all, help prophets to work with apostles.

Apostles and prophets

This is the biblical pairing for anything that is broader in its geography than a local congregation, and even for ministry within the local church where that is possible.

Scripture tells us that this pairing is the foundation of the church, with Christ the cornerstone. Scripture never puts pastors and prophets together in the same way. The Bible tells us that God has put in the church first apostles, second prophets. And by the way, 'pastor' does not even appear in that listing. Eight times in all this pairing appears in Scripture.

The prophet is made in such a way that he needs the authority and government of the apostle. He can submit to authority in others, but sooner or later for the ministry to be released and received in God's way it needs the counterweight of the apostle. Prophets without apostles are loose cannons and can end up firing in the wrong direction. Apostles without prophets can easily be blind to God's direction and strategies.

How does the apostle-prophet pairing work in practice?

The problem is that there are so many dimensions and permutations, all we can do here is catch a glimpse of some of the possibilities. And sometimes even these roles can be exercised by both prophet and apostle. In essence prophets will 'see' direction, foundations that need to be laid, or foundations that have been laid and are wrong. They will see strategy and function. Prophets will see gifting and will see people who are stuck like square pegs in round holes. Prophets can facilitate the dynamic of the Spirit.

The apostle is the builder, the collector of information and the provider of a blueprint or plan.

As noted earlier, it's as if the prophet is up a tree and can see above the people below. He can see miles ahead and can see the direction to take and the things that may lie along the way.

The apostle will give directions: who should do what, and how to handle the obstacles that lie along the path.

One thing I know is that both need each other. To translate these roles into the terms of Belbin's team profiles, which you may be familiar with, the prophet is like the Belbin 'plant' and the apostle is like the Belbin chairperson. Plants cannot function properly without a chairperson doing their job.

I have worked with some disengaged, even dis-illusioned prophetic people over the years. In nearly every case they do not have an apostolic friend or co-worker who can help them through the inevitable turmoil that goes with the territory. Or if they do have such a person, the relationship for some reason has become tense or even estranged.

I have had several such friends and colleagues. Dave Richards, Jim Swihart and Jonathan Booth have been friends who have worked at seeing this pairing operate.

What are the keys they hold?

- They have opened doors for me
- They have challenged me when they feel I am out of order
- They have worked to help finance or pray in finance for initiatives that I have been involved in with them
- They have believed in the gift I carry
- They have looked for ways for that gift to be used and have put people and resources behind it
- They have not used the gift or the relationship for their own ends
- They have drawn from me and taken notice of what I then contribute
- Where they have deemed what I bring to be of God they have endeavoured to implement it
- They have encouraged me to take time out to have fun and to work with them
- They have set aside time for productive work and friendships as a result of these relationships
- They are keen to see me develop in character and in gifting

The interesting thing in my mind is that there has never been a question of who had the leadership – each of the three would feel totally comfortable in correcting or shaping me, but each of them is also open to receiving correction and adjustment. There are corresponding, albeit very different, strengths in our gifting. They clearly lead in their areas, but there is no hint in these three of one-way leadership.

Someone asked me how I have the capacity to deliver some quite radical messages, even provocative at times, yet have managed to stay linked in to church leaders. The inference being, surely you run the risk of being estranged?

The answer to that question has a number of facets:

I believe it is clear in 1 Corinthians 14 that prophets should be consistently open to have their words and their knowledge weighed. That is a settled issue for me, and something that is wanted, not just tolerated.

Another key is that I trust these apostolically gifted men. I do believe they love me and want the best for me. I also trust the ministry that God has placed in them. That's not foolproof, and there are times when we have had strong disagreement or we have agreed to disagree, but in principle it's not difficult to work with leadership like this.

Another reason is that because of their friendship and the dealings of God over the past three decades, I am more secure these days in my gifting and am more comfortable to have things challenged.

I asked a friend this week a question which I would like you to reflect on: What is more important, truth or love? Perhaps I should say, what is more important, knowledge or love?

It's a fascinating question, because a prophetic person will often be very protective over their word (their truth or knowledge). It's at this point that 1 Corinthians 13, the famous love chapter, kicks in:

> If I have the gift of prophecy and can fathom all mysteries and all knowledge ... but have not love, I am nothing. (1 Cor. 13:2)

Love here includes having a genuine love for the recipient of the word you bring. But another expression of love is relationship. And if I am so intense with my word that I am not prepared to have it weighed or to have apostolic gifting work with me on it, then I guess I am nothing!

If you have a prophetic ministry, I encourage you to pray for this pairing in your life if it doesn't exist – and if it does exist now, or comes to you in the future, can I encourage you to nurture the relationship and give it your best shot?

How does it work for the apostles?

In Scripture, and in today's churches, apostles typically work with teams in new church planting and in handling the issues, concerns, doctrines and practices of existing churches.

What is it that prophets bring to them in their spheres of responsibility? I asked Dave Richards and Jim Swihart for their thoughts. First, here are some of Dave's thoughts.

The apostle needs the prophet

- to see the task strategically
- to motivate the workers to begin the task
- to maintain that motivation to continue that task
- to help the apostle complete that task
- to declare the ultimate purpose of the task at hand

The book of Haggai clearly shows this, with the Temple having been at foundation level for fourteen or fifteen years of inactivity. The prophet Haggai prophesies to Zerubbabel, an apostolic type, and to Joshua, the High Priest, and the work is done. After seven prophecies in four years they go from foundation laid to roof on! Haggai prophesied it would be this way over a three-and-a-half month period.

It is also clear in Ephesians 2 that apostles and prophets lay foundations together, and in Ephesians 3 that they move together in revelation as to the mystery of Christ and God's plan for the church.

In short, if Amos 3:7 is correct and the Lord God reveals his secrets to his servants the prophets, the apostles need to be connected to the prophets, because they build more steadily and have a better sense of putting the purpose of God into place in order to get his will done, not just the inspiration that it's time to do the job!

One result for me is that I know a difference in the Spirit when I am teamed with prophets. There is a sharing of the load and a real sense that you are yoked together for a purpose.

Jim approached the same thing from a different angle. Here are some of his thoughts around the value of prophetic input:

- It saves you from taking short cuts in appointing new leaders
- It saves you from expediency in appointing elders
- It saves you from making rash decisions
- It helps you maintain sound doctrine and a balanced diet
- It helps you maintain biblical standards of holiness
- It keeps you to an outward focus
- It challenges us to seek his kingdom rather than building the church
- It helps prevent major splits
- It helps us to deal with the problem of a 'square peg in a round hole', i.e. a prophet trying to be a pastor
- It challenges you to have a prophetic vision for the church
- It challenges you to define it
- It challenges you to prepare for its implementation
- It challenges you to divide it into its various departments, each with its own vision

- It challenges you to carefully select those who should govern the part
- It challenges you to start preparing leaders for the future
- It helps you to guard the spiritual environment of the church
- It helps with counsel and wisdom on gossip and broken or strained relationships
- It helps you not to run away from your problems
- It helps you to be disciplined in delegating
- It challenges you to move in the supernatural and take risks
- It ensures room is made for all the Ephesians 4 gifts
- It ensures good foundations are laid in church plants
- Working together to accomplish a task is much more effective than trying to do it all ourselves

To summarise the value of this pairing, the prophets see what God is doing and the apostles take responsibility to implement and build what the prophets see.

Prophets and teachers

This pairing appears just once, but in an important setting. In the church at Antioch – a thriving, sending, Spirit-enabled church – prophets and teachers met with the apostles and prophets for fasting and prayer to seek God for strategy and direction. It was this grouping that was the seedbed for emerging apostolic gifting.

In 1 Corinthians 12, teachers are third in the list of giftings that are said to be appointed by God.

Why would this pairing have significance?

I can tell you that from my point of view, teachers are the greatest asset to me in applying the plumb line of the Word of God. If I want to check a sensing or a word theologically or biblically, I share it with my teacher friends. Weighing a particular word or a direction that I am sensing from the Spirit will give me exposure to the breadth of Scripture and a view of whether what I think I am hearing is in harmony with the written Word of God.

How do these two equipping ministries work with each other in practice?

They clearly work together in my experience. The prophet will lay a foundational word, an insight or a revelation that triggers a deposit that's already in the teacher.

My teacher friend Tony Gray put it this way: 'Sometimes I have something in me, and a prophetic word opens the valve so that what is deposited can flow out.'

The teacher acts as a reservoir, built up through many years of reading books and being soaked in Scripture. The prophet acts like running water, which bubbles up out of the ground and then disappears. The teacher gathers this up into the reservoir.

For Tony, it works on a number of levels. In a gathering, any prophetic word that has been shared can be added into the mix of what is being taught.

On a broader theme, prophetic books or prophetic words with a broad application will act as a provocation and a stimulus. The teaching gift will sift and order (this fits with that) and provide the church with a more consistent stream of understanding.

Prophetic people will wisely share with teachers and ask, is what I am saying getting the right reaction in you, does it match, is it in harmony with Scripture as a whole?

It's a powerful partnership that runs both ways, in that the teacher will pick up tendencies for divergence and the prophet acts to provide the stimulus that the teacher is in tune with what is the bubbling word from the Spirit for now.

Summary

- Churches should always be led by a team
- Pastors and prophets complement each other's roles
- Apostles and prophets complement each other's roles
- Apostles and prophets are the normal biblical pairing
- Apostles and prophets are foundational roles for church growth
- Teachers and prophets complement each other's roles

Action Moment

If I could sit with you now over a cup of coffee I would ask what two or three things most impacted you as you read the book. I can't, but the moment has arrived for some action. If you would find this helpful, I will suggest a couple of questions for you to answer and would encourage you to make some commitment to the first steps.

Action point 1
What three things have most impacted you as you have read this book?

1. ....

2. ....

3. ....

Action point 2
What three actions will you commit to as a result?

1. ....

2. ....

3. ....

Action point 3
Who will you share this with, and by when?

1. I will go and share this with ....

2. I will do it before ....

We would love to know where the Spirit of God has stirred you, and would also love to know how things grow and develop as you put some of these ideas or principles into practice. Please do contact us at help@insight-marketing.com to tell us some of your story.

Appendix 1

Old and New

A number of people have asked me to include in this book some brief pointers about the differences between the Old and New Testaments regarding prophets and prophecy. I am indebted to Bible teacher Mike Beaumont for his help here.

The similarities

In both Old and New Testament times there were forms of prophetic activity outside the realm of God's people. In the ancient world there were diviners, ecstatics, clairvoyants, mediums, astrologers and sorcerers. All these were fairly common, but they were forbidden by the law (Deut. 18:9–13).

In the New Testament similar occult phenomona were common. There were shrines where the gods were consulted for spoken counsel and guidance. The oracle at Delphi, for example, was world-famous: cities and nations consulted the prophetess for her answers. Prophetesses known as Sibyls were especially popular in Rome, their writings predicting wars, famines, the rise and fall of nations, etc. Soothsaying and sorcerey were seen in the New Testament, for example the slave girl at Philippi who had the spirit of divination (literally, 'the python'), and Elymas (his name means sorcerer), who in Acts 13 had to be dealt with by Paul with blindness as he sought to oppose the gospel. In both cases Paul dealt with the occult spiritual force working through them.

The differences

In the book we have seen that the promise for our generation was to be different from the scope of prophetic activity in the Old Testament. In those days, apart from just a handful of notable exceptions, prophecy was for the select few. In the New Testament it's for everyone, including children. In Acts we see at least ten different applications of this variety. This is the new breadth that was promised by Joel and reaffirmed by Peter.

What does this transition mean? The prophet is no longer quite the central player that he was in the Old Testament. In the Old Testament the prophet was a key force in holding kings to the covenant. Now Jesus is the King and we are called a nation of kings and priests. There was also little written of the word of God in the Old Testament period, but of course in the time of the early church the whole of the old is written down and the New Testament writings are on their way. In the New Testament the apostle bursts onto the scene with strategic emphasis and he is seen to be the key player.

A new plurality

Plurality is one of the differences between the Old and New Testaments. In the Old Testament, prophets often appeared alone, although there was a degree of plurality in the numbers belonging to the schools or companies of prophets. In the New Testament, this takes on a new dimension. It is to be apostles and prophets working together alongside pastors, teachers and evangelists. As we saw in chapter 14, the plurality of these flexible teams is at the heart of New Testament prophetic function. There is a quite specific importance placed on the teamwork of the apostles and prophets.

A new purpose

A change of emphasis occurs. With no kings to challenge and no exiled nation, the purpose of the New Testament prophet takes on a new shape:

- It is to bring encouragement, edification and comfort
- It is to instruct believers (an element of teaching)
- It impacts both believers and unbelievers
- It is built on the written Word of God; it is not creating the written Word of God
- It includes predictive warning and apocalyptic applications

Appendix 2

Prophetic Development Toolkit

A: Creation journal

Fill in the columns that are relevant for each object. Don't worry if there are blank columns. The idea is to learn to record what you see instinctively, and then to help develop your senses to observe more than is apparent at first glance. Use a separate sheet to record anything else that might be striking or interesting. When you next ask God for a word, see if some of these observations help to enrich it.

Object
Colours
Shapes
Contrast
Feel
Smell
Movement
Emotion
Size
Texture
Background

Appendix 2

Prophetic Development Toolkit

B: Workplace or home journal

Fill in the columns that are relevant for each object. Don't worry if there are blank columns. The idea is to learn to record what you see instinctively, and then to help develop your senses to observe more than is apparent at first glance. Use a separate sheet to record anything else that might be striking or interesting. When you next ask God for a word, see if some of these observations help to enrich it.

Object or event
Other people
Colours, environment, clothing, etc.
Contrast
Feel
Smell
Movement
Emotion
Size
Texture
Background
Shapes

Appendix 2

Prophetic Development Toolkit

C: Leadership matrix

Helping those who prophesy to develop and grow

Use this prophetic development tool in conjunction with the weighing matrix (Appendix 2 D). Before using it, please refer to chapters 5, 6 and 10.

As you hear the prophetic word, ask yourself the following questions and jot down your answers.

1. How do I summarise what I am hearing?
2. What is the heart content of the word?
3. How does it fit with any other words or scriptures so far?

4. What are my feelings just now?

5. What track record does this person have with us?

6. What are my feelings as I face my responsibility to weigh this? Am I nervous or defensive?

7. If I am to give an honest and authentic response, what is it going to be?

8. Is it directional? If so, what am I going to do with it now?

9. Is any response necessary?

10. If a response is necessary, how will I express that now?

Before you use the weighing matrix (Appendix 2 D), please consider the following:

a. What would a 10 out of 10 prophecy look like to me?
b. What would an ill-timed prophetic word look like?
c. How would I know if the spirit in which it is given is good, poor, or a mixture?
d. How can I serve this individual and the gift in them?
e. What are the most important two or three things I can communicate to them now?

Any other thoughts or observations:

Now ask the prophet whose word you have weighed the following questions:

a. Please score my feedback out of 10, where 10 is high or good and 0 is low or very unhelpful.

b. How could my feedback have been more helpful?

c. How well-received do you feel by the leaders in this church, especially with regard to your gift? (Score out of 10.)

Appendix 2

Prophetic Development Toolkit

D: Weighing matrix

Score each aspect out of 10, where 10 is high and good, and 0 is very low and rather bad! Any written comments next to each category scored would be really appreciated.

	Score	Comments
Timing In the flow of the meeting, was the delivery at the right time?		
Effect How well did it encourage, edify or comfort?		
Delivery How appropriate was the style of delivery?		
Clarity How clear and understandable was the word? (If it was woolly, score low.)		
Fit How well do you believe it fitted with the meeting's direction?		
Length Was the length of the word about right?		

	Score	Comments
Spirit Was the prophet's spirit good?		
Focus How well did the prophet avoid drawing attention to themself?		
Agenda Did the prophet keep clear of any hidden agenda?		
Mixture If the prophecy was just about 'all God', score 10; if you felt there was human addition, score lower.		
Personal Was the prophet free of insecurity, reaction and frustration?		
Accuracy Particularly for personal words: how accurate was any detail? (If not applicable, write N/A.)		

Additional comments: Any specific ideas for learning, improvement and encouragement? In your opinion, how could this word have been better delivered?

For extra copies email enquiries@insight-marketing.com

Appendix 2

Prophetic Development Toolkit

E: Prophetic variety

Using the list below, give yourself a score out of 10 (where 10 is high) according to how closely you feel your particular expression of prophecy matches that of the named biblical figure. Those that you rate with a score of six or more could give you a glimpse of some of the variety that lies within you and your gifting. You might like to have your church leader, friend or spouse do the same exercise on your behalf.

Abel prophesied through his workplace.

Joseph dreamed and could interpret the dreams of others. He had a strategic and administrative application to his gift.

Miriam took a tambourine and led the women in dancing and spontaneous singing.

Moses performed miraculous signs and wonders, and did awesome deeds with mighty power. He knew the Lord face to face. He wrote and sang songs.

Deborah brought military strategy to the nation through her gifting. She was an amazing motivator.

Samuel heard the audible voice of God and was set aside to serve God. He confronted kings. He engaged in symbolic or dramatic acts, including pouring out water before the Lord.

A group of prophets, presumably in Samuel's training school, played lyres, tambourines, flutes and harps.

Elijah confronted the prophets of Baal with a supernatural contest. Three times he was fed by miraculous supply. He performed miracles, including raising a dead child and calling down fire from heaven. Elijah was an intercessor.

Elisha performed miracles. A widow was saved from destitution when he got her to bring pots and pans that were subsequently filled with oil. He raised a young boy from the dead. He neutralised poison in a communal dinner. He fed a hundred people from twenty loaves. He could see into the heavenly realms.

Nathan was a wise man, a person of insight and a military advisor to the king. He confronted the king over Bathsheba with a parable.

Gad, along with Samuel and Nathan, kept written records.

Ahijah ripped his cloak into twelve pieces on meeting Jeroboam.

Isaiah walked naked and barefoot for three years as a symbolic act. He called on the Lord successfully to make the sun go back ten steps.

288 sons of Asaph, Heman and Jeduthun were set aside for the ministry of prophesying, accompanied with harps, lyres and cymbals.

Shemaiah and Iddo, one a prophet and the other a seer, kept written records and worked with genealogies.

Ezra and Haggai were inspirational preachers.

Jeremiah made a yoke out of straps and crossbars and wore it to depict an impending Babylonian bondage. He watched a potter at his wheel and used the scene as a prophetic metaphor. Jeremiah also sent prophetic letters.

Ezekiel did some modelling and then laid a mock siege. He lay on his left side for 390 days and on his right side for 40 days. He was grabbed by his hair and given insight into the heavenly realms.

Daniel was a strategist, a wise man and a member of the main political think-tank of his pagan government. He dreamt and could interpret dreams. He had supernatural encounters with angels and angelic princes.

Hosea was commanded to marry a harlot and name each of his three children as a prophetic statement. He prophesied judgement with great literary richness.

Joel, Amos, Obadiah, Jonah, Micah, Nahum, Habakkuk, Zephaniah, Haggai, Zechariah and Malachi prophe-sied the future in different ways, using an amazing variety of literary content.

Agabus prophesied symbolically with a belt which he put around Paul.

Barnabas was one of a small group called prophets and teachers. He was an encourager, but also a prophet who would seek God with a group for church planting strategy.

Judas (Barsabbas) and Silas were preachers and encouragers.

John was a mystic and an apostle, who wrote down the amazing revelation he had seen, rich in symbols.

Appendix 3

Resources from David Oliver for Churches and Businesses

Churches

If you are interested in organising a one-day prophetic development workshop or a dream workshop with David Oliver and team, please email enquiries@insight-marketing.com or call 0870 7877404.

Address:

Insight Marketing
Cricket Corner
Lynch Hill Park
Whitchurch
RG28 7NF

'Love Work, Live Life' and Care for the Family: national events

Care for the Family runs regular workplace events with David Oliver. For full details of their national evening programmes and their sector-specific national events call 029 2081 1733 or visit www.careforthefamily.org.uk and look for events.

Keynote talks for business

If you are interested in having tailored training or change management or a keynote speech in your business on a range of topics, including:

- Leaders or managers – which should we be, and why?
- Work-life balance for improved profitability
- Stress and learning – the difference between the clock and the compass
- Marketing
- Sales skills
- Negotiation

Call 0870 7877404 or email enquiries@insight-marketing.com

Business resources

Training

David Oliver has trained in excess of 100,000 people worldwide and specialises in in-house training and keynote delivery in:

- Negotiation
- Sales
- Strategic customer care
- Closing more sales
- Gaining high-value clients through innovative marketing
- Leadership

For more details email enquiries@insight-marketing.com or call 0870 7877404.

For a list of audio training resources on CD please visit www.insight-marketing.com/cd_library.htm

Outsourced marketing functions
For information on outsourced lead generation and marketing clinics please visit

www.insight-marketing.com

Amazing family or corporate experiences on a yacht

For family or corporate packages on a 36-foot yacht, please visit www.yachtsforfun.com

Mike Madden, a reader of one of David's books, took his three sons for a weekend on Cool Runnings, the 36-foot yacht. He says, 'Having never sailed before, it was great fun and very rewarding for the four of us under the guidance of an expert skipper to learn new skills, face fresh challenges, and just take time out to be family together.'